Edward Lear as a Landscape Draughtsman

Zante, 1848 (1857).

Edward Lear as a Landscape Draughtsman

by PHILIP HOFER

The Belknap Press of Harvard University Press
Cambridge, Massachusetts
1967

To F. L. H., without whom I might have been as lonely as Edward Lear.

Preface

IT IS NEVER EASY to write a foreword to a book that has otherwise been finished. Either one tends to write at too great length on extraneous matters, or to make one's acknowledgments sound too factually cold and thus unappreciative. Moreover, this book is only an introduction to the subject of Edward Lear's landscape watercolors, drawings, and sketches which surely will be dealt with at greater length either by one of my successors or by one of my colleagues, like Brian Reade, who could write with a different perspective. Nor is this volume a catalogue of the Harvard Collection, which is still growing slowly. And least of all is it intended to deal with the artist's oil paintings or his nonsense drawings, which last form a very distinct group in themselves of the highest importance to the study of caricature and graphic humor.

The hardest part of the preparation of my material has been sorting out the Harvard drawings, which were certainly in as great general disorder as when they were left in this state (undoubtedly) by Lear himself! Next most difficult was to ascertain the present whereabouts of Lear landscape drawings, due to the wide dispersal of them over the past thirty-six years, at rising prices. The fashion for Lear "watercolors" as they usually are called — although few of them are properly precisely that — is very great at the present writing. And there is no evidence of a weakening in public interest: rather the contrary, as the full stature of Lear, the writer and man as well as the artist, becomes clearer. It is my opinion that he is altogether one of the leading British nineteenth century figures, because he had so many different facets to his genius, even though he was quite conservative in some particular ways. Lear, as a letter writer and creator of nonsense verse, is recognized. But Lear, as a poet, has not begun to be properly studied. Lear the traveler has been almost forgotten. Lear's psychological personality will undoubtedly attract some present day psychiatric "authority," and I profoundly hope he will not be "psychoanalyzed" into anything but the adorable, humorous, loyal, creative, shy, hardworking man that he was! In my view he deserves all happiness in his posthumous reputation to compensate for the little recognition his genius received from the bulk of his contemporaries and his immediate successors.

Meanwhile, I wish to acknowledge with warm thanks varied and valuable information from the following colleagues. In England, from my friend Angus Davidson, Lear's biographer; from John Lowe, Director of the City Museum and Art Gallery at Birmingham, and from Brian Reade of the Victoria and Albert Museum particularly; also from Mrs. Vivien Noakes, of Reigate, who is about to write a work on Lear herself. Information regarding specific Lear collections came from Mrs. Mary E. Millett, the Earl of Derby's librarian at Knowsley; from Alan Gouk, of the Fine Arts Department at the British Council in London; from the Director of the City of Lincoln Libraries, Museum, and Art Gallery; from my friend Edward Croft-Murray, curator of the Department of Prints and Drawings in the British Museum in London; from Hugh MacAndrew of the Ashmolean Museum at Oxford; from my friend Keith K. Andrews of the National Gallery of Scotland at Edinburgh; from J. H. Morley, Keeper of Art in the City of Leicester Museums and Art Gallery; from Miss Ann Clements, Art Assistant at the Whitworth Art Gallery in Manchester; from Martin R. F. Butlin, assistant keeper, the Tate Gallery in London; and finally from Robin Campbell, Deputy Art Director, The Arts Council of Great Britain in London. Private individuals and collectors also responded to my inquiry, notably the Lord Bridges, the Lord Strachie, and the Lord Tennyson as well as my friends Sir Steven Runciman, Osbert Lancaster, Geoffrey W. G. Agnew, John P. Baskett, W. Plomer, Mrs. Charlotte Frank, Miss Yvonne ffrench, and Philip James. Finally, David Markham, Mrs. Robert Hollond, L. G. Duke, Professor Paul Thompson, Edgar C. Behrens, Stephen Harrison, and Lady Gillies gave me data on their personal collections. Indeed Lady Gillies went even further: she gave me the addresses of her relatives in New Zealand which enabled me to reach Craig Gillies and John A. Gillies, who so notably helped me with information about Lear's collateral descendants who have Lear drawings. Many previously unpublished drawings are reproduced in this volume with the permission of Mr. Franklin H. Lushington.

I am indebted to Raoul de Broglie, Conservateur-Adjoint du Musée Condé at Chantilly in France; to Miss Eleonore Schonfeld, Acting Librarian of the McGill University in Montreal, Canada; and I am very particularly indebted to my friend Francis R. Walton, Director of the Gennadius Library at the American School of Classical Studies in Athens, Greece, who gave me almost all the information I have about Greek collections and collectors.

In the United States, of course, I owe great debts. Special thanks are due to my colleagues and friends John Walker, Director, and J. Carter Brown, Assistant Director of the National Gallery of Art in Washington; also to Andrew C. Ritchie, Director of the Yale Art Gallery; Herman W. Liebert, Director of the Beinecke Library; Donald C. Gallup, a curator in the Yale University Library and the leading Lear collector in America that I know, although his colleague at New Haven, Professor Michael Coe, helped me and shows great promise too. At Princeton, my friends Gillett Griffin, Professor E. D. H. Johnson, Professor Charles Ryskamp, and Professor William Shellman have helped me. At Smith College, my friend Charles Chetham, Director of the Smith College Museum of Art, told me of two drawings there. Further West, I have corresponded with my friends and colleagues Harold Joachim in the Art Institute of Chicago; Henry S. Francis in the Cleveland Museum; and especially with Robert R. Wark, Curator of Art in the Henry E. Huntington Library at San Marino, California, whose exhibition in November and December 1962 and its cat-

alogue did much to spread an interest in Edward Lear on the Pacific Coast. Francis P. Farquhar, an old friend in San Francisco, also wrote me about his Lears.

In New York, I should particularly thank George A. Dix of the Durlacher Gallery, another old friend, who has allowed me to acquire some of my own best drawings; also my friend and colleague Jacob Bean, Curator of Drawings at the Metropolitan Museum of Art, and Gabriel Austin, Secretary of the Grolier Club. John Brett-Smith, President of the Oxford University Press in America, is an old friend who released the text of Section I in this book, first published as their keepsake in 1962. Dr. James S. Murphy was very helpful about his late brother Ray Murphy's fine collection of Lears; and thanks to the catalogue of the Davis Galleries' late autumn, 1966, exhibition of Lear drawings, I learned about one or two collectors with whom I was not in touch.

Dennis Farr, Curator of the Paul Mellon Collection at Upperville, Virginia, wrote me about the Lears which are there, and hinted at Lears to come to this same amazing trove of British paintings and drawings. As we now know, this collection may go before long to Yale University in New Haven.

In my own area, Boston and Cambridge, and in Meriden, Connecticut, I owe the largest debts of all. To E. Harold Hugo and William Glick of The Meriden Gravure Company, I am indebted for much help with drawings that "would not fit the page" and the quality of the reproductions in this book. Mrs. St. John Smith, a long-time colleague and friend, told me of the four drawings in the Boston Museum of Fine Arts, while Miss Agnes Mongan, one of my closest colleagues, told me of the Fogg Museum drawings at Harvard, one of which I had forgotten I gave to them myself! And I owe my friend Dr. Charles P. Lyman, Research Associate at Harvard's Museum of Comparative Zoölogy, the name for the small animal (*Hyrax capensis*) Lear "drew" on April 13, 1832!

I cannot estimate what I owe to the officers and employees of the Harvard University Press — the Director, the Production Manager, editor, designer, typists, and delivery boys. But I do know that I owe Miss Eleanor M. Garvey, Assistant Curator of the Department of Printing and Graphic Arts in the Harvard Library, and Miss Carolyn Jakeman of the Houghton Library, and my secretary, Miss Susan Kashiwa, my profound thanks for all their help and patience. Miss Garvey and Miss Kashiwa read proof and made corrections while I was in Europe from March through May, 1967.

Cambridge, Massachusetts   PHILIP HOFER
26 June, 1967

Contents

I. A Short Biography
    of Edward Lear   1

II. The Tradition of Landscape Drawing
     That Lear Inherited   6

III. Lear's Technical Procedure in
      Landscape Draughtsmanship   11

IV. Development of the Artist
     as a Draughtsman   15

V. The Relation of Lear's Drawing
    to His Painting   49

VI. An Estimate of Lear as a
     Landscape Draughtsman   52

VII. The Growth in Appreciation of
      Lear's Landscape Drawings   59

VIII. Present Status of
       Lear Collections   63

IX. A Short Bibliography of Works
Relating to Lear's Landscape Drawings 72

List of Plates   77

Plates

Edward Lear. From a photograph taken in Rome, ca. 1860.

A Short Biography
of Edward Lear

I

IN 1938, ANGUS DAVIDSON, a then young British author, wrote an illustrated biography of Edward Lear, now regrettably out of print, which was so successful that no one has attempted another since. Instead, it was reissued as a Penguin paperback in 1950. It is not laced with dry-as-dust statistics, but is a living story, filled with quotations from Lear's letters, diaries, journals, and the remembrances of his contemporaries. Anyone who really wants to know Lear the man, as well as Lear the writer and artist, should refer to this book, but a shorter outline of his life and personality here may not be out of place. Without one, it would be more difficult for any new reader to assess his genius, even if it should be admitted at once that Lear tried to keep his life and his very strong emotions separate from his poetry, nonsense, sketching, drawing, and painting.

Briefly then, Edward Lear was born in or near Highgate, on the outskirts of the city of London, May 12, 1812, and died at San Remo, on the Italian Riviera, January 29, 1888. He was one of the youngest children of Jeremiah Lear, a well-to-do stockbroker, whose (naturalized Danish?) grandfather may have changed his name from Lør to an anglicized phonetic spelling. His mother, Ann Skerrit Lear, was English — with fifteen children (out of twenty-one!) who survived childbirth. The artist's own account of their large house, Bowman's Lodge, and their twelve carriages, has recently been questioned, as has the story of the family's subsequent ruin and his father's imprisonment for debt in the King's Bench Prison. Nevertheless, it is reasonably certain that the shy, hypersensitive youngster, with myopic eyes and a nose too large for his pale face, began to earn his living at an early age by drawing for shops, doctors, and hospitals. He is supposed also to have colored fans and prints, and to have painted screens, but the writer has never been privileged to see any of these. A much older sister, Ann, had a small income, £300 a year, inherited from a relative. She it was, rather than his parents, who answered his very personal emotional needs, from his childhood until her death in 1861. Until he was twenty she also furnished him a home.

With our contemporary interest in psychiatry, we are led to suspect, given the undeniable fact of Lear's emotional insecurity, that at least some of his respiratory troubles and his asthma were psychosomatic in origin. His severest illness of all, which he suffered from the age of seven, almost certainly was. In the thirty volumes of his personal diary, which is at Harvard, he frequently refers to it as "the Demon," and marks the many seizures, taking place mainly at night, with an "X." Were these a light form of epilepsy — what the French call "petit mal"? Angus Davidson, the biographer of Lear, thinks so. In any event, here, more than in his family's middle-class origin, its financial trials, and his lack of formal education, may be found the main cause of his continual anxiety, his need to dramatize his problems, his lack of con-

fidence, and, above all, his constant, wistful loneliness.

On the other hand, it would appear from other evidence that basically Lear must have had a strong constitution, for few artists or writers have been more hardworking or productive. He learned to write and speak adequately seven languages, including ancient and modern Greek, Arabic, and Albanian. He also lived to be nearly seventy-six years old at a time when this was more than a normal life span. And, still more notably, he spent a large part of his middle fifty years constantly traveling in countries and remote provinces where housing and sanitary conditions were extremely primitive at this period. With very little money, he led a life that many a twentieth-century traveler would find unsupportable, but, with all its difficulties, greatly to be envied.

One fortunate early meeting did much to make this life possible. In 1830 or 1831, while sketching at the London Zoo in Regent's Park, he was introduced to Lord Stanley, son of the twelfth Earl of Derby (1752–1834), who owned a private menagerie at his country estate, Knowsley Hall, near Liverpool. He also met Lord Derby himself, who wanted an illustrated description of his birds and animals and hired Lear to make it. Employment turned into friendship when the Earl discovered that Lear was entertaining his grandchildren every evening with highly original nonesense stories, rhymes, and drawings. The formerly rather homesick artist was, thereupon, encouraged to remain at Knowsley Hall for four years and to become almost a member of the family. From that experience and success, he was able to make influential friends as would not then have been conceivable without an introduction to a prominent member of the one social group in Europe best fitted and able to support him. Soon he came to realize that this specific patronage had changed the entire course of his life, and he remained eternally grateful.

Yet partly because of the conventional character of Victorian society, Lear was never quite happy in England or with the aristocracy in general. He began to chafe at society's demands, at boredom, at those "swells" he grew to call "brutes, porchi, apes, and owls," while the damp, cold winters depressed him and gave him influenza and asthma. So from 1836, when he was only twenty-four, Lear managed to obtain enough commissions and to sell enough paintings and drawings to a wide assortment of people — a few Americans included — to travel or live abroad, simply, over the next half century. In 1837 he discovered Italy for the first time, and he continually returned throughout his life. The numerous colonies of British residents there offered him work and enlarged his circle of friends. Then he visited, or sometimes lived in, the Ionian Islands, Greece (his favorite country from a scenic point of view), Turkey, Albania, Dalmatia, Serbia, Malta, Egypt, the Sinai peninsula, Lebanon, Jordan, Palestine, Syria, southern France — and even far-off India and Ceylon.

In spite of close friendships retained in England, his return visits to his native land became steadily less frequent. His last stay was in 1880, nearly a decade before his death. But throughout his life he kept up with his friends at home and abroad by constant correspondence. One can learn much from his letters, and they make wonderful reading. They are by turns keen, philosophic, gay, and sad; they are nearly always spiced with nonsense words or drawings. To the poet Tennyson, then on the Isle of Wight in the early days of their friendship, he wrote characteristically: "Do you think there is a Pharmouse or a Nin somewhere near you where I could paint quietly" (he suffered from noise of *any* kind) "and come to see you and Mrs. Tennyson promiscuously?" The nonsense in this letter was not banter: it was an apology to a new friend for a request that he thought might otherwise seem too bold, and it was a cloak for his selfconsciousness.

The fact that Lear never married may be considered another poignant testimonial to his shyness. Although he had early vaulted into friendship with the aristocratic world of England's diplomats and travelers — and this feat of manners, personality, wit, and intelligence during the unbending Victorian period should not be belittled — he felt too diffident and humble to inflict himself permanently on a woman. He also considered himself to be quite hopelessly ugly. He knew that he was sloppy in habits and dress. Anxious beneath his parade of whimsy, he deprecated his volatile moods and also greatly dreaded exposing his epileptic attacks. Psychiatrists would have a fine time with Lear's diaries, since even a cursory study of them reveals a desperately insecure man constantly harassed by hypersensitivity and worry. They also show that he was at least twice in love. On both occasions he drew back at the last moment, even though he would seem to have had a good chance of being accepted. It is unlikely that Lear was a homosexual although he was very emotional about his male friends. He had, for example, a consuming desire for intimacy and unrestrained communion with Franklin Lushington, a taciturn, cold, undemonstrative judge, married and ten years his junior, which reveals an adolescent or perhaps slightly feminine element in Lear's character. Perhaps one can evaluate these contrasting attitudes best by suggesting that they indicate an unstable, contradictory temperament swept by ever-changing moods.

Toward the end of his life, Edward Lear traveled much less than in earlier years. Although he had only recently passed sixty in 1873, his fourteen-month tour of India and Ceylon with his friend Lord Northbrook — then the British Viceroy — depressed and exhausted him. He had executed over fifteen hundred drawings during this expedition. From then on he realized he must curb his roving tendencies, and he began to live permanently in San Remo on the Italian Riviera — earlier at the Villa Emily and later at the Villa Tennyson. The first of these villas may have been named after his close neighbor and friend Emily Tennyson (or perhaps after a great-niece in New Zealand); the second was certainly named for the Poet Laureate. Thus it is clear that his desire for a "Pharmouse" near the Tennysons turned out to be prophetic.

Eventually he ceased to wander at all, except around northern Italy and southern Switzerland in the warm season. The last long entry in his diary (Tuesday, August 2, 1887) contains a whole page about his failing health, his lack of appetite, the doctor's visit, and so on. He feared that he was threatened with heart failure or paralysis. Meanwhile, both the Tennysons were a constant comfort to him. So too was his faithful manservant Giuseppe, a successor to Giorgio Kokali, the Albanian who had attended him for twenty-seven years. Until the last few months of his life, Lear also had the companionship of his venerable cat "Foss" (often spelled "Phoss"). Sadly he wrote its epitaph, and a measure of his growing weakness lies in the exaggeration of Foss's age, actually seventeen, which he claimed to be thirty-one! Once he had buried Foss in his garden, he lost the will to continue his daily diary entries. Indeed, he had almost stopped several months before.

The final entry in Lear's diary, however, which the writer has only once before quoted in print, is for Monday, December 5th: "Dreariness . . . [yet] out of doors bright sun. Looking over journals for 1887. Weary work

. . . I shall try to get some sleep if possible, but I have no light or life left in me, — and the flies are as horrible as ever." By contrast, when he died the following month (January 29, 1888) of heart failure, his end was peaceful. Lear's life was an unending series of ups and downs.

There will not be space, nor is there justification, to write about Lear as a literary figure in this book. Yet one must remember the literary is the far more fully appreciated side of his genius. Even though few people have read his travel books, and fewer still the serious poems like "Cold are the Crabs" — first published in *Teapots and Quails* (1953), from the manuscript now at Harvard — the whole world knows Lear's limericks, and such nonsense poems as "The Owl and the Pussycat," which, despite obvious difficulties of translation, has recently been translated into French. Lear's humor was essentially childlike — which is of course the reason he could enchant children till the end and could appeal to the youthful spirit that lurks in adults. As David McCord, the poet, perceptively notes: "Lear's humor was never a lance, pointed. It was not a weapon; it was his shield." Surely that fact becomes poignantly clear as soon as one reads any of his nonsense songs and stories.

Finally, if one has ever been lonely oneself, has ever worried long and fruitlessly, one grows to love this shy, humorous, bumbling man who tried so little to exploit the world, and put so much back into it. In spite of his asthma, epilepsy, weak eyes, the rheumatism he contracted in the wild regions he visited — often without adequate clothing or cover — this man without money, wife, or child, traveling ceaselessly, far from home, managed to invent hundreds of new word forms, to write dozens of poems and humorous essays, to popularize the limerick, to dash off or carefully compose up to thirty-five letters a day; to write, illustrate, get published, and largely sell by mail and by subscription seven travel books; to illustrate three considerable natural history volumes completely and many others (such as John Gould's *Birds*) in part; to write and illustrate four published books of highly original nonsense; to write the music and to sing a number of songs; and painfully to fill in, day by day, perhaps as many as sixty volumes of diaries and an uncounted number of journals. All this he did in addition to making thousands of paintings, watercolors, drawings, and sketches, some of which are more fully described in the following pages. And, finally, he made literally hundreds of friends, the closest of whom remained his intimates for life.

This, gentle reader, is *achievement*!

The Tradition of Landscape Drawing That Lear Inherited

II

ONE WOULD LIKE TO BE ABLE to claim that Edward Lear was as original in his chosen career of peripatetic landscape painter and draughtsman as he certainly was in the field of nonsense. But this would not accord with the facts. Although very engaging and prolific, he was a late comer in the long tradition of British traveler-artists who followed the flag to the far corners of the world — a tradition beginning, perhaps, with John White (fl. 1585–1593) when he joined Sir Walter Raleigh's second expedition to America in 1585. Or with Inigo Jones (1573–1652), who went to Rome in 1603 or '04 and again in 1613–14 — although one must concede that Inigo Jones was not primarily a designer of landscapes but rather of architecture and of fête scenery and costumes. A little later in the seventeenth century, the naturalized English artists, Sir Anthony van Dyck (1599–1641) and Wenceslaus Hollar (1607–1677) made romantic watercolors and topographical views — to differentiate the one from the other — of great beauty. And, finally, Thomas Manby, who flourished between 1670 and 1695, worked in Italy several times. It was because of these more important Tudor and Stuart artists, and a few lesser ones, that a British taste for the natural scenery of foreign lands began.

But the eighteenth century fashion for the "Grand Tour" to Italy was a much closer and stronger influence on the artistic atmosphere in the British Isles which influenced Lear to become a landscape painter. Encouraged by travelers' reports and by such significant books as

Robert Castell's *Villas of the Ancients* (London, 1728), Palladio's *Fabbriche Antiche* (London, 1730, dedicated to Richard Boyle, third Earl of Burlington), and *The Architecture of Palladio with Notes by Inigo Jones* (London, 1742), the British aristocracy began to cast their eyes towards the warmer climate and romantic beauty of Italy. The constant wars with France had ended at the death of Louis XIV in 1715. Then, suddenly, the classical art treasures of Herculanaeum, near Naples, buried deeply by the great eruption of Vesuvius in A.D. 79 so vividly described by Pliny the Younger, were rediscovered in 1738, and a wave of excitement about archaeology swept all over England and France. Giovanni Battista Piranesi's *Prima Parte di Architetture* (Rome, 1743) hailed the still greater monuments of the Roman Empire's capital. In no time at all, a rush to Italy was on.

As might have been expected, artists participated as soon as they were able. Alexander Cozens (1717–1786), a natural son of Peter the Great of Russia, was probably in Rome for a short time before 1742 and certainly was there in 1746, so he can be called the first important British artist of this era to work in Rome. Richard Wilson (1714–1782), who actually lived there for seven years between 1749 and 1756, painted and drew far more. He was the first Englishman to be strongly influenced by the classical tradition of the great seventeenth century continental artists, Claude Lorrain, Nicholas Poussin, and Salvator Rosa. In Italy, he found it was not necessary to search for the "picturesque," which through-

out the eighteenth and part of the nineteenth century was such a fashionable preoccupation, because its elements were an integral part of every view near Rome! There were always classical ruins, the distant mountains, the blue Mediterranean or Adriatic sea, lakes, stone pines and cypresses. When Wilson returned to England, in the later 1750's, he brought an enthusiasm for the Italian atmosphere and the Italian point of view which Canaletto had also encouraged after his arrival in England for a visit in 1746. No wonder, then, that a score of other important English artists took the long road to Rome before the year 1800, and that a number more went on from there to the South and to the East, as Lear was to do later on.

Two of the most exciting English travelers who journeyed eastward were Robert Wood and James Dawkins, spurred on by the "Society of Dilettanti," formed in 1733–34. Wood and Dawkins were not artists, however, but travelers and archaeologists; the artist who accompanied them in 1751 by way of Rome, Naples, Athens, the Greek Isles, Constantinople, Asia Minor, Syria, Palestine, and Egypt, was Giovanni Battista Borra, an Italian from Turin. Still, they brought back his sketches, and their own, from which developed two wonderful folio books, *The Ruins of Palmyra otherwise Tedmor in the Desert* (*sic*; London, 1753) and *The Ruins of Balbec* (London, 1757). These books created a sensation.

Equally important, meanwhile, were the British artist-architects James Stuart (1713–1788) and Nicholas Revett

(1720–1804) who had also had the encouragement of the "Dilettanti." Wood and Dawkins record finding Stuart and Revett at Athens in 1751, making measured drawings on the Acropolis. But Stuart and Revett's *Antiquities of Athens* appeared a little later (London, 1762). When it was published, it gave still another spur to the public taste, inducing the "Society of Dilettanti" to send a still better landscape draughtsman, William Pars (1742–1782), to Greece for two whole years, 1764–1766, in order to aid in the preparation of their *Ionian Antiquities*, the first part of which they published at London in 1769.

Most influential of all, perhaps, in the formation of the public taste was Robert Adam (1728–1792), a really important artist who began his "Grand Tour" in 1754. Moving on from Italy to Dalmatia in 1757, he was accompanied by a French landscape painter, Charles Louis Clérisseau, whom Adam later prevailed upon to stay in England from 1771 to 1778. Through their collaboration on this trip came what is perhaps the single most beautiful English travel book of the eighteenth century: *The Ruins of the Palace of the Emperor Diocletian at Spalatro in Dalmatia* (London, 1764). Now England had contributed a large share of archaeological publications, and this last folio had fine landscape engravings as well. Although these particular plates were mainly due to Clérisseau, what is rarely cited in the literature about Adam himself is that Clérisseau and Piranesi, between them, influenced and released this great architectural innovator's imagination. Later in life (about 1777 to

1787) Adam made some relatively fantastic and delightful watercolors in which architecture and romantic landscape mingled just as they did in Piranesi's greatest engravings.

By this time, a second wave of British artists had already started its sweep over France and Italy. John Robert Cozens (1752?–1797), son of Alexander Cozens, John Skelton (died in Rome 1758), John (called "Warwick") Smith (1749–1831), Francis Towne (1739?–1816), Thomas Rowlandson (1756–1827), John Downman (1750–1824), and Joseph Wright "of Derby" (1734–1797) — these are among the eminent English artists who made the Grand Tour of the later eighteenth century memorable by their landscape drawings. But even these were not yet the immediate forebears of Lear. Nor were those artists who ranged farther afield like William Hodges (1744–1797), the draughtsman in Captain James Cook's second voyage to the South Seas, and William Alexander (1767–1816), who went to China with Lord Macartney's embassy in 1792. More immediately comparable to Lear, because more contemporary and more closely related to him in point of view, were George Chinnery (1774–1852), who worked in India and China from 1802 till the time of his death, and the three Daniells: Thomas (1749–1840), William (1769–1837), and Samuel (1775–1811), an uncle and two nephews who stayed for long periods in India and Ceylon between 1785 and 1794. These three artists are said to have used the "camera obscura" (as Canaletto did) to obtain topographical accuracy, and theirs was the tradition which Lear was to inherit when he himself finally went to India and Ceylon with Lord Northbrook in 1873–1875, nearly a century later, on his last adventuresome drawing expedition.

A third wave of British artists traveling abroad left England in the first thirty-five years of the nineteenth century — still a little before Lear. This period was called "The Golden Age of English Water-Colour" in the introduction to a 1958 British Museum Drawing Exhibition catalogue. Thomas Girtin (1775–1802) and Richard P. Bonington (1801–1828), despite their youth, were the leaders of those who stayed in or near Paris. But Joseph M. W. Turner (1775–1851) proved in the end to be the most important Grand Tour landscape artist of all. Despite the fact that he traveled to the continent as early as 1802 and then again and again till 1845, he remained essentially English and became the greatest non-continental European landscape painter and draughtsman of the whole nineteenth century — with the possible exception of John Constable (1776–1837), who never left his native shores. Lear really cannot be compared with Turner except in his love of travel, for in the widely developing character of his watercolors and in the variety of his abilities Turner greatly exceeded his humbler admirer and successor.

John Sell Cotman (1782–1842) was more like Bonington and Girtin in his aims and his geographical range than he was like Turner. And Samuel Prout (1783–1852), although really not a landscapist in the sense that Lear was, achieved one of the greatest reputations of the English water-color school in the nineteenth century. Prout went to Normandy and to the Rhineland as early as 1819–20.

We now come to the landscape draughtsmen who were of Lear's own generation or whose lives most closely paralleled his own. Thomas Shotter Boys (1803–1874) should perhaps be mentioned first, because although he lived nearly as long as Lear, he disappeared from prominence about 1845, when Lear was only just coming into his own. Boys may possibly have been a pupil of Bonington. In any case, he worked near him in Paris as early as 1825, also traveling to Belgium and possibly to the Rhineland and Spain, making sketches and watercolors in which an architectural interest was greater than a feeling for natural scenery. (With Lear, of course, landscape came first.) William Callow (1812–1908) was in Paris with Boys from 1831 to 1834; he considered Boys an "eccentric" — a possible explanation for Boys' virtual retirement during the last thirty years of his life. Richard Dadd (1819–1877), who traveled to the Levant in 1842, certainly was eccentric if not mad, and spent his later years in Bethlehem Hospital, but continued to be artistically productive. Francis Danby (1793–1861), a native of Ireland, came to London in 1813 but later left because of domestic difficulties; from 1829 to 1841 he lived near Lake Geneva and traveled as far afield as Norway. John Frederick Lewis (1805–1876) and William James Müller

(1812–1845) traveled still further; Lewis to Spain in 1832–1834 and to the East in 1839–1851; Müller to Italy in 1833–34, to Greece and Egypt in 1838, and to Asia Minor in 1841. James Holland (1800–1870) was also an able British watercolorist of the period, who visited France, Switzerland, Italy, and Portugal. But probably nearest to Lear in purpose, in achievement, and in artistic viewpoint, were David Roberts (1796–1864) and James Duffield Harding (1798–1863).

Roberts, a Scotsman from Edinburgh, was distinctly the greater artist of the two (he became a member of the Royal Academy, which Harding and Lear did not) because he was more original in his watercolors (of three distinct coloristic periods) and his outlook. Several of Roberts' books became famous, including his *Picturesque Sketches in Spain* (London, 1836–37), and particularly his *Holy Land, Syria, Egypt, and Nubia* (London, 1842–49), a great six-volume folio work which ranks with the greatest color-plate travel books of any period. It is, in fact, greater than any single one of Lear's own. Roberts went to the continent in 1824, but at that time remained, as most of the other English artists did, mainly in Belgium and Northern France. Then in 1832–33 he went to Spain and Italy; in 1838–39 to the Near East and Egypt. His watercolor landscape drawings of this period are usually more atmospheric than Lear's, but some are very hard and cold. Towards the end of his life, unlike Lear, Roberts lived and worked in the British Isles.

Harding, for all his versatility and his enterprise, was a lesser figure than either Roberts or Lear. He was a good teacher, but as a draughtsman did not measure up to the others. He often, indeed, contented himself with making lithographs after other artists' work. Such were his *Views of Pompeii* (London, 1828), after William Light, and his *Subjects from the Works of R. P. Bonington* (London, 1829–30). There were a few good original works of his own, however: *Sketches at Home and Abroad* (1836), is cited by Thieme and Becker's *Künstlerlexikon*. Yet as these perceptive German art-historical compilers were impelled to write, Harding's "industry exceeded his creative powers."

While Roberts, Harding, and Clarkson Stanfield (1793–1867), a still lesser figure, were Lear's principal artistic rivals, they had none of his literary powers. And Lear never permitted himself to notice them, just as he even more pointedly ignored the very existence of Lewis Carroll (1832–1898), his somewhat younger rival in the field of nonsense. In fact, Lear ignored all his competitors; for throughout his active life he remained desperately insecure. As far as his career in landscape painting and draughtsmanship was concerned — his principal livelihood — he had some reason to be. Living far from England, without family there, or any powerful artistic representative or agent, he always ran the risk of being forgotten. He was almost forgotten, in fact, within a few years of his death.

Lear's Technical Procedure in Landscape Draughtsmanship

III

AMONG THE ALBUMS OF LEAR DRAWINGS at Harvard, willed by the artist to Sir Franklin Lushington, his heir and executor, is one which contains a number of very early sketches. These are of all types and subjects, but one is of special interest here. It is a finished watercolor drawing of a small animal (*Hyrax capensis*) in the margin of which Lear has "doodled" a self-portrait pencil sketch. Below he has written: "Sketched at 17. Drew . . . April 13, 1832." Lear was seventeen in 1829, and in the pencil sketch, drawn full face, he is already wearing spectacles!

Lear's drawing and note are important. First, they prove that his early difficulties with his eyes were probably not wholly psychosomatic. Second, they show that he had already begun a procedure which he continued with few variations to the end of his life: to make a quick pen or pencil sketch (with careful color, texture, and other pertinent information) while he was in the presence of his subject and to elaborate it later, either on reaching home or on some other day when he could not (or did not care to) sketch in the open. How much later the elaboration took place is not often revealed in writing as it was in this case, but his diary shows that he was continually at it. Until his last twenty years, the time lag was ordinarily not very great. When it was considerable, he usually noted the fact. Regularly after each sketching tour in foreign parts he would shut himself up for weeks on end to elaborate his drawings while his impressions of particular scenes were still vivid. Sometimes he then signed and dated his drawings all over again, either copying the penciled dates or adding new ones when he felt he had made a mistake. This elaboration, or more rarely compression, of his landscape sketches is the process he so often referred to in his diary entries as "penning out." (He had a psychological need, as well as an ability, to be steadily occupied when he was alone.) Sometimes he erased his old penciled notes, but more often he left them in, and even sometimes copied them in ink. Then he brushed colors or tonal washes over the whole composition rather freely, except where he planned a finished drawing for some client. In the latter case, all the notes were removed and the drawing was refined and "polished" like his smaller paintings. The "free" drawings were generally for his own reference collection, as a basis for the finished commissioned drawings and oils.

There is nothing unusual in this method. Before 1850 it was standard procedure in England to make sketches on the spot and then to finish them later indoors. Being by nature a traditionalist, Lear naturally formed all his habits unusually early, and he then usually adhered to them grimly — even after most other artists changed to newer ways. Lear clung to all the early Victorian concepts by instinct as well as because of his abiding pride in the fact that he had given drawing lessons to the young Queen herself. Thus he remained essentially a conservative always, even when failing eyesight (which was always "failing" — one eye did eventually go almost completely) caused some noticeable alterations in his style. With this single exception, his basic approach, once achieved, remained constant. Lear was not an innovator like Alexander Cozens or Turner. He did not, except on very rare occasions, attempt pure watercolor. He was essentially a draughtsman, working in line, who colored his drawings in the manner that has already been noted.

In the preface to Lady Strachey's *Later Letters of Edward Lear* (London, 1911), Lear's younger friend and erstwhile drawing pupil, Hubert Congreve, vividly describes the way his mentor set to work when they went on sketching expeditions together, "Lear plodding slowly along, old George (his servant, Giorgio Kokali) following behind, laden with lunch and drawing materials." When they found a good subject, "Lear would sit down, and taking his block [of paper] from George, would lift his spectacles, and gaze for several minutes at the scene through a monocular glass he always carried; then, laying down the glass, and adjusting his spectacles, he would put on paper the view before us, mountain range, villages, and foreground, with a rapidity and accuracy that inspired me with awestruck admiration. Whatever may be the final verdict on his 'Topographies' (as he called his works in oil or water colour) no one can deny the great cleverness and power of his artist's sketches."

To this picture, Brian Reade of the Victoria and Albert Museum in London adds the following comments in his excellent introduction to a catalogue of the Lear Exhibition of 1958 (The Arts Council of Great Britain): "[Lear's] subjects descended from preconceptions fashionable in the period of Martin and Turner, but his technique as a water colourist went even further back, to the 'stained drawings' of eighteenth century masters like Towne, though his style, unlike theirs, was impulsive. He seldom attempted direct water colour painting in the manner of Peter de Wint, which was practised everywhere by the time he reached middle age. If he could have escaped a little more from the canons of taste prevailing when he was a boy he would have been a different person of course, but he might have made an excellent Pre-Raphaelite . . . In his own topographical specialty his vision and technique were based on the transitional Neo-Classical-Romantic conventions applied to 'dramatic' or 'picturesque' landscape."

Finally, to these better publicized British statements, Robert R. Wark, an American, added the following observations which also deserve quotation. They are to be found in his introduction to an exhibition catalogue (1962) of the Henry E. Huntington Library and Art Gallery, San Marino, California: "Lear kept a large stock of . . . working drawings in his studio. They were shown to prospective customers, but when the customer had made a choice, Lear was apparently less likely to sell the original drawing than he was to execute another based on it . . . Certainly [these may] lack some of the freshness and spontaneity of the initial sketches, but they nevertheless retain all the basic qualities of Lear's style."

These three comments on Lear's procedure are so pertinent that they have been quoted at some length even though they may be familiar to readers of this book who have studied Lear's drawing. While looking at the reproductions in this volume the reader should notice the wide technical range between the shorthand of Lear's on-the-spot sketches and the minute detail of the highly finished drawings which he made for sale. The other drawings, in various stages of completion, were returned to boxes, to large wooden cabinets (two of these are at Harvard), or to trunks, or were pasted into albums, with numbers down in the lower corners for the indexes which Lear nearly always forgot to make, or misplaced, or lost.

Certain subjects were delineated again and again. Thus at Harvard there are many drawings and a painting depicting the citadel of Corfu — from different distances, from varied points of view, and in different lights (with a preference for sunset), only a few of which can be reproduced in this volume (plates 41, 61, 107, 108a and b). In them the sea is almost always as calm as a mill pond, the profile of the citadel sharply outlined against the sky. It must have been in this aspect that Lear admired it most; for he repeated it many times, over many years, up to the final months of his life. Perhaps it was something personally symbolic; at any rate, he drew it again and again, on paper of every conceivable size and shape. He repeated many other subjects, too, but no others are so frequently represented in the Harvard collection. Mount Athos may have been another symbol to him, but the language of his symbolism — and there almost certainly was one, as with William Blake — has yet to be deciphered. (Again and again certain subjects and exaggerations appear in Lear's nonsense drawings — long noses, for instance — which can only relate to subconscious, if not conscious, anxieties.)

Unquestionably Lear's drawings, at the start, were intended to furnish him with subjects and data for his finished drawings and paintings. Since he did not consider that finished drawings by themselves could either furnish him a living or satisfy his higher ambition, paintings for which a much larger price could be asked were "necessary" for his livelihood and his pride. Drawings simply assisted him on the road. He held "eggzybissions" of them in whatever gallery he found available, in the places where he lived abroad, in London, or at home when he finally had his own villa at San Remo. Sometimes he gave away drawings (particularly "nonsenses," which were not competitive with his main profession) in hopes of commissions to come or as thanks for hospitality received. But far more frequently in later life he sold them singly or in groups as chance offered, and they became, perhaps without his realizing it, all-in-all the greatest occupation of his life. In his last years he also sought and obtained more commissions for drawings than he did for paintings; as he had regretfully discovered, his large paintings did not sell. His final years were spent almost entirely on designs for a projected illustrated edition of his friend Tennyson's *Poems*, which he drew and redrew over and over again.

Besides Lear's manuscript diary (a stock cloth-bound octavo volume which the firm of Letts, in England, supplied to him every year), the artist kept a certain number of manuscript journals, usually on larger paper. Most of these have "disappeared," as Angus Davidson has recently advised me. It is possible that after Lear's death some of them were sent by Sir Franklin Lushington to New Zealand, where the main group of the artist's collateral descendants had settled, but of this we are not certain. Lushington mentions them in an appreciation of Lear that he wrote for *Macmillan's* (the magazine) in April 1897. He also says there were "Notebooks" concerning the drawings. But these last I can find nowhere else more than fleetingly recorded. Did Lear burn them, as he seems to have later burned the diaries he kept at Knowsley Hall between 1832 and 1836, because they contained matters too intimate even for Sir Franklin Lushington, his closest lifelong friend, to see? We may never know. But, in any case, these "lost" notebooks, journals, and manuscript diaries (other than the Indian Journal and the diaries for 1858 to 1887 included, which are now at Harvard) could be of the greatest importance for further study of Edward Lear as a poet, as an artist, and as a human being. And I have a feeling that some are hidden away in England. Perhaps Mrs. Vivien Noakes, a very intelligent young woman who is planning to write on Lear, will discover them.

Development of the Artist
as a Draughtsman
IV

EDWARD LEAR'S PROFESSIONAL CAREER falls naturally into three periods so far as his landscape drawings are concerned. For simplicity's sake they may be titled and dated as follows: (1) Youth, about 1827 to 1847; (2) Maturity, 1847 to 1875; (3) Old Age, 1875 to 1888. But for convenience the middle period should perhaps also be divided into three parts: 1847–1852; 1853–1873; and 1873–1875.

Of course some readers and critics may not wish to concede that a man who has reached thirty-four — Lear's age in 1846 — is still a youth; and others may maintain that sixty-three is not old age at all! Still, for Lear, these dates are reasonable. One must remember that he settled on the career of landscape painter only after he left Lord Derby at Knowsley for London in 1836, his eyes strained by the exacting detail of natural history drawings. He was already twenty-four then, and yet a comparative neophyte at the art of landscape, as his English Lake pencil drawings show. During the next eleven years he formed his personal style in his new profession. As for his twenty-eight years of maturity, they need no explanation or excuse, since his drawings prove a continuing competence the whole time. After Lear's return from India on January 29, 1875, he had reached another turning point in his life. He was an old man in his psychological approach to life and to adventure. Gone was the will to travel beyond the relatively narrow confines of Italy, Switzerland, Corfu, and England. His weariness also becomes apparent through the fact that his work dwindled in both quantity and scope. Age is a comparative matter, but there is no doubt that in Lear's case it began soon after he reached his home, with the trip to India behind him.

Youth: 1827–1847

Long years before his return to the Villa Emily in 1875 but well after Lear had grown up and achieved a little success, he occasionally talked about his early days in a shy, self-deprecating manner. There is little doubt that he exaggerated his hardships when he said that he "began to draw for bread and cheese at the age of fifteen" (1827). With his oldest sister, Ann, who had a small independent income, to fend for him it probably was not *quite* that bad! On the other hand, his further comment that his first efforts were "uncommon queer shop sketches" rings true. A small quarto album full of just the sort of rather highly colored flower, fruit, bird, insect, fish, and seashell drawings that one would expect to find at a shop was in his residuary estate at San Remo. It was willed to Sir Franklin Lushington and is now at Harvard. A few of the drawings in this earliest lot may be by Lear's sister Ann, since one of them is actually signed "A. Lear," but the majority are doubtless his own, although few others are signed. A number of drawings contain writing in his hand. Thus on the back of a "Fritillaria Meleagris," in color, is a delicate pencil drawing of two toadstools, with the following information in Lear's autograph: "This vegetable pro-

duction I found, May 1, 1828, on [*sic*] a flower bed, etc." It is the earliest dated Lear drawing of which the writer is aware. This drawing and the rest of the album show that Angus Davidson was right in reporting in his biography that when Lear was able to go out into the country at this time, "he would occupy himself in making minutely detailed drawings of birds, butterflies, and flowers."

The next dated drawing at Harvard is equally slight. It is the one referred to at the beginning of Section III — a small pencil self-portrait, inscribed "Sketched at 17." Actually, this is no more than what is popularly called a "doodle," just above a much larger finished watercolor of a somewhat homely rodent-like creature (*Hyrax capensis*) which is the part of the whole composition that he "Drew" (i.e., completed) three years later on April 13, 1832.

Thus far I have seen no true *landscapes* by Lear that can be dated 1829 or earlier. But very soon thereafter comes a group of tiny pencil sketches on a single quarto leaf contained in another album now at Harvard (plate 1a; 9 x 9 inches). Because this sheet of pencil drawings is pasted on the back of another leaf containing some pencil and watercolor studies of a parrot dated "August 1830" in Lear's hand, one guesses that both groups of sketches were made at the same time. A very closely similar parrot is in the upper left-hand corner of this sheet of pencil sketches, while pen studies of its feathers trail off to the right. To be cautious one should perhaps not date them at all, but they are almost certainly before 1832, when Lear's *Illustrations of the Family of the Psittacidae* was published in London. All the drawings in this particular album relate to that (Lear's first) great book. Therefore, they can probably be claimed to be among the earliest of his true landscape drawings so far recorded.

The watercolor "Javanese Peacock" (plate 1b; 9 x 7 inches), is dated "1831" on the lower left, and signed "E. Lear" on the lower right. It comes from another small square quarto album at Harvard, also measuring 9 x 7 inches in the original. A very delicately tinted, romantic background of rocks and tropical vegetation accompanies the peacock, and similar backgrounds appear with some other flower and bird studies in the same album. But this is about the only type of landscape Lear attempted, as we shall see, until he changed from being an ornithological draughtsman to his preferred career as a landscape painter.

The original drawing for the lithographic landscape signed E. Lear at the bottom and reproduced on plate 2 (9 1/2 x 10 inches) is probably from the same time as the Javanese Peacock, since it was used for the cover of one of the original parts of the *Psittacidae*, which must have been prepared before the book itself was complete. It certainly has similar elongated palm trees and highly imaginary scenery, within a framework only slightly larger. But neither the Javanese peacock nor the *Psitta-*

cidae cover compares with the splendid watercolored "Antelope" to be seen on plate 3 (9 x 8 1/4 inches), even though the landscape background remains much the same. Faintly, in the left-hand lower corner of the antelope watercolor, one can make out "Febru 7," but no year. This time one might guess 1832; for the antelope is placed close in the larger album to the *Hyrax capensis* which we have already seen Lear sketched in 1829 and completed in 1832.

Now, having spent a good deal of time with the very earliest slight drawings, I must move more rapidly through a few odd drawings at Harvard which are not very exciting, but happen to be signed and dated. This fact gives them a significance beyond their aesthetic qualities. They are, in a sense, technical landmarks for judging other drawings which cannot be so accurately placed. Plate 4 (3 1/2 x 5 1/4 inches) reproduces, slightly enlarged, a small pencil landscape inscribed "Burpham, October 3. 1834," which is the earliest dated (though not signed) true landscape by Lear in the Harvard Library collection. Next, "Umbrellifera, Kendal, August 20th, 1836" (plate 5; 4 1/2 x 6 5/8 inches), unsigned, comes from an entirely different small album also from the Lear bequest to Lushington. The album, given by the writer to Harvard, has been broken up into its individual manuscript contents. This small pencil drawing anticipates Lear's "nonsense botany" titles, but is much earlier in date. The figures are handled passably well, but in style they resemble those of many other English artists who "drew for bread and cheese" at this period. One would not notice this drawing, really, but for the date.

Now, at length, we come to some full-sized, more interesting landscape drawings. The first in sequence at Harvard is a pencil drawing inscribed "Rydal Water" and is dated "7 Oct. 1836" (plate 6; 7 x 10 1/4 inches). Even though this may actually have been drawn after Lear had made his decision to become a landscape painter, it is rather unsure, especially in regard to the trees. Its virtue lies in indicating, for the first time, that Lear had a pronounced gift for topographical outline. Did the artist really make ninety-three or more landscape drawings on this trip? (See the number in the right-hand lower corner just above the date.) The chances are that he did. Throughout the whole of his long life, Lear's large output proves him to have been always exceedingly industrious, while his diary shows that habits once acquired were seldom changed. A number of other pencil drawings from this trip to the English Lakes are to be found in collections both in England and America — and probably some from an Irish trip in 1835 as well.

As has already been related, Lear set off for Italy early in the summer of 1837 on his first trip to the continent of Europe. A pencil drawing, "Luxembourg. July 20th, 1837" (plate 7; 6 1/2 x 9 3/4 inches) indicates the route he planned to take. Looking carefully at the drawing, which is on gray paper, we notice that this time he splashed some highlights of Chinese white in the foreground and in the sky. In all but this last respect, however, "Luxembourg" is technically close to the view of "Rydal Water" drawn nine months earlier, although there is a little more firmness in the handling of the middle ground. What is more importantly new is the respectable handling of the architectural elements, suggesting that he had made other drawings of this nature before. We wonder, then, why he tended to subordinate architecture as he grew older. In this connection, please notice the next reproduction (plate 8; 10 1/2 x 7 1/4 inches), inscribed "Frankfurt (am-Main), 25 August 1837." This is really wholly architectural and even more competent. One is reminded at once of the work of Samuel Prout and of Thomas Shotter Boys, Lear's immediate predecessors in this style of architectural rendering and in the treatment of the townfolk's "regional" costumes. Clearly Lear was eclectic at first in imitating these better-known artists so closely, and that he could have rivaled them if he had pursued this interest is more than likely.

"Zürich, 26th Sept. 1837" (plate 9; 10 x 14 inches) shows still other technical improvements, but no significant change in style. The use of Chinese white for the highlights continues and has become more frequent and more vigorous. The calm water of the lake is perfectly expressed in pencil shading even without color. And other drawings of 1837 are much the same. "Genzano di Roma" above Lake Nemi (plate 10; 10 1/2 x 14 3/4 inches) was probably drawn soon after Lear reached Rome and is in the same technique and spirit.

We must now jump a whole year, to "Tivoli 28 Sept. 1838" (plate 11; 12 x 17 1/2 inches), in order to find a further development in Lear's power. Still entirely in pencil, trees that were stylized and conventional before have become the most important and strongest element in the scene. Moreover, they seem to be *particular* trees, for all their romantic wildly spreading branches. Thus early Lear proved his love of olive trees — a love that he never lost. One has only to look at the large oil sketch (plate 106; 18 x 23 inches) of olive trees (on the island of Corfu?) — which was made much later in his life — to be convinced of this point. It was the one tree Lear used most for his foregrounds, although he loved to draw other varieties of trees, too, in the linear grotesque attitudes of old age (plate 14; 16 x 9 3/4 inches).

The much less finished pencil sketch of "Isola Farnese 1 April 1840" (plate 12; 11 x 17 1/4 inches) contains an early example of Lear's written directions to himself in the foreground: the words "rock," "dark clear," "olives," "meadows," etc. This device, as we have seen, early became an almost unfailing habit of Lear's for all his first studies of subjects that he intended to develop later on as finished drawings or oils. (So far he apparently did not see fit to use phonetic spelling, although it would be quite unwise to conclude he had not yet thought of it.) In all drawings earlier than 1840 that we have seen so

far, these instructions have been erased — if they were employed at all, which is something we do not know! Although "Tivoli," of 1838 (plate 11), not much further completed than "Isola Farnese," has no written notes, "Nemi, 12 October 1840" (plate 13; 10 1/4 x 16 3/4 inches) carries them, as does a view of St. Peter's from the Pincian hill terrace above the Piazza del Popolo (plate 15; 11 1/4 x 17 1/4 inches), which has been tentatively dated 1841 by Bertha Coolidge Slade in *Lear on My Shelves* (New York, 1933), the largest of all existing Lear catalogues (made for W. B. O. Field).

Another pencil drawing, inscribed "Isola San Giulio, Lago di Orta, 1842" (plate 16; 9 3/4 x 13 1/2 inches) shows a progression both in time and in approach, but has no directions; it may have been drawn for sale. This is the first instance among the dated drawings at Harvard in which Lear reveals a definite interest in atmospheric effects. All the earlier drawings have had clear sky, with light clouds (usually drawn in Chinese white) or no clouds at all. Here on the Lago di Orta a heavy rainstorm is plainly indicated as it pours over the meadows at the left. The lake is smooth as ever, the people and objects are incidental, but the drawing is on light blue paper, instead of on gray. On the other hand, "Palermo, 16 April 1842" (plate 17; 9 1/2 x 16 1/2 inches) has almost no atmospheric feeling at all.

The first complete technical change to be seen in the Lear drawings at Harvard is in the view of "Passerano

20 October 1843" (plate 18; 7 3/4 x 15 inches). This is actually a watercolor, made with a brush and freely but delicately shaded in various hues from the purple and lavender hills in the distances to the grays and browns in the fortress and the pastel greens and olive in the foreground towards the right. That this is not a "finished drawing" on commission or for sale is indicated by the fact that pencil notes have not been erased but just washed over. Nevertheless, it is a drawing that has perhaps been "penned out," with no indication when this secondary and very freely washed elaboration was done. Because the place and date as well as all the principal outlines in the composition have been copied by pen on top of the original pencil lines, one assumes that the time is substantially the date of the pencil sketch beneath; for usually Lear added a second date when the time lag was considerable. The "penning out" may have been done on the spot. This watercolor of "Passerano" has a noticeable stylistic and geographic as well as a slighter technical relationship with "Santa Rosa di Conca, June 8, 1844" (plate 19; 12 1/4 x 20 1/4 inches) and a number of other somewhat later drawings at Harvard which are in about the same stage of completion.

What is exciting in all this group is that Lear seems suddenly to have become interested in broad tonal effects. To be sure, "Santa Rosa" has only shades of brown wash added for this purpose, in the eighteenth century "tinted" manner, all over the center of its composition and up into the sky, to give a subtle indication of clouds. But the general tonal effect is the same as in the "Passerano" watercolor. And Lear employed another new device in the "Santa Rosa" brown-washed drawing; that is, he drew in first a preliminary sketch of the buildings on the lower left, which are worked out in more detail for the finished composition. To prove that this was not an isolated case, the writer owns a somewhat smaller pen and wash drawing of "Santa Rosa di Conca" from a different viewpoint, made on the very same day, which uses this identical technical device to outline, in a few strokes, the artist's idea for the whole composition. Lear went on experimenting in this manner for a year or two more, and then seems to have abandoned the device before it became a habit. Or else thereafter he made the small outline sketches on a piece of scrap paper and later threw them away. Quite a number of such small outline sketches are reproduced in the text of Lady Strachey's two volumes of Lear letters.

A shaded pen drawing (with no wash added) of "Amalfi, 9 June 1844" (plate 20; 17 1/4 x 10 3/4 inches) has a similar kind of sketch showing a peasant's heavy-set figure (far up on the left) which may be an enlargement of one of the men to be seen struggling along the twisting road to Ravello in the left foreground of the main drawing, as well as a small preliminary sketch of a building. But much more important than these technical devices is the fact that the last two drawings show greatly improved draughtsmanship. Compare this strong "Amalfi" and the "Santa Rosa di Conca" with the drawing of "Rydal Water," or "Luxembourg," and see how much certainty, vitality, and strength Lear had achieved in the seven years that had passed since he first set out for his new career on the continent.

Equally competent is the pen and brown wash drawing of "Ponte Sant' Antonio 1 May, 1845" (plate 21; 11 1/4 x 19 inches). Indeed, it is about as powerful an unfinished drawing as Lear ever achieved! He was almost thirty-three years old. Again notes in pencil and in ink abound, but now phonetic nonsense such as "rox" (instead of rocks) appears for the first time. And probably "raven," in the right foreground, stands for "ravine" (why should there be a crow at that spot?). Quite possibly Lear's nonsense "stream of consciousness" began at the same time that his first *Book of Nonsense* (London, 1846) was being prepared. In 1845 his mind must have already begun to work on nonsense actively as well as subconsciously. Further evidence to this same effect is quite easy to find. "San Vittorino 2 May 1845" (plate 22; 11 x 18 inches), is full of it: "Rox and Dox" are the two most conspicuous words in the right foreground, while the words "O! path!" actually do climb up the path to the monastery; and "clumps of Holives" (for olives) is

written twice in the middle ground in the left, once in pen and once in pencil. Since "raven" also appears, in the center foreground, a very logical place, we once again assume it means "ravine." And Lear has made several sketches of the distant mountains in outline on the side.

Clearly now Lear's youth was passing and his maturity was about to begin. For we find every evidence of his full competence, and all his continuing favorite devices, in the drawings last mentioned. To be sure, he may have abandoned the frequent use of tonal washes during 1846 after the publication in that year of his Italian travel books (which also employed them), for we do not see them reappear in the drawings of 1847. It is a pity that they don't; since he used washes very well. But we find only slight improvements from now on, instead of the rather rapid jumps in competence that can be observed in the previous illustrations. Certainly Lear learned later to handle his incidental human figures more convincingly and deftly. He changed his color scheme from brighter colors to pastel shades. He also later trained himself to render distant outlines still more adroitly. But the main areas of his ability and his style had been formed. Henceforth, we will be dealing with an artist who was the equal of all his contemporaries in topographical skill. He was not their equal in atmospheric effects, and never would be. Nor did he ever attain the gift of portraiture.

It is, however, within his own self-imposed limits that we must judge him. What he *wanted* to do, he did well. And no one could ever persuade him to try what he did not feel he *could* do well. His sense of insecurity pursued him into the deepest reaches of his artistic nature.

Maturity: First Period, 1847–1852

We jump now two years in time, and from Italy to Sicily, without finding much change in Lear's technique or style beyond his abandoning tonal washes. "Modica. 7.8.June 1847" (plate 23; 9 1/2 x 13 3/4 inches) is perhaps more simply and easily constructed, through shorthand drawing, than "Ponte Sant' Antonio" or "San Vittorino," but the only new element is the addition of penciled figures in the upper foreground, after the preliminary pencil drawing had been "penned out." Lear, at this point, began to make more of an effort to study human and animal forms, which were incidental to his main scenes, with a growing realization of their value in giving his landscapes scale and life.

"Melazzo 3 July 1847" (plate 24; 14 x 19 3/4 inches) and "Zante 30 April 1848" (plate 25; 10 x 14 3/4 inches), for "penned out" preliminary studies, are close to the approach and style which Lear was to maintain for many years to come. He had abandoned the rich brown washes he had used so effectively in 1844–45 — a practice that may have had special reference to the large two-volume *Illustrated Excursions in Italy* he was then preparing for

publication, which had tinted lithographs giving somewhat the same effect. When this work was published (London, 1846), he had no more immediate reason to work in this manner. Rather, he reverted to a more linear type of multicolor washed drawing, when he worked in color at all, than the watercolor of "Passerano" (plate 18) made in October 1843. And that he did so with increasing frequency will be revealed in the drawings of 1848 and 1849 to be seen in the next reproductions.

"Athens June 5.6. 1848" (plate 26; 11 1/2 x 19 3/4 inches) is a case in point, for it is rather fully colored although its washes are still nearly as free and loose as those of "Passerano." But the figures in the foreground are sizeable (like those in "Modica"), not tiny as in so many earlier drawings. To see the Theseion in open country with a herd of sheep in the right middle ground may well surprise the reader who knows the Athens of modern times. The Plaka district, however, lies on the left, almost as crowded as it is now, and the Acropolis, for all that the drawing shows at least one old Turkish watch tower that no longer stands, is as fully dominating as everyone now sees it. This is a drawing with a little more "atmosphere" than most. Right next to the date, Lear has left his penciled note, "Hymettus misty." So when he "penned out" the mountain of that name, he used a mixed gray and lavender wash. The figure on muleback closest to the observer has a Prussian blue waistcoat; otherwise the colors are all soft and subdued.

The next view of Athens is more surprising (plate 27; 11 1/4 x 17 1/2 inches). It is the earliest but by no means the only *night* scene in the collections at Harvard. "Penned out" so thoroughly and so darkened with heavy gray and brown washes that nothing more than "Athens — 5. 9 10 p.m. 1848" can be faintly made out of the title on the lower right, and even this requires the aid of a magnifying glass. Chinese white has been used to brighten the fragments of marble columns in the foreground (on the Acropolis near the west portal of the Propylaea) as well as to pick out a few human figures and sheep in the middle ground, some of the city lights, and a rift in the heavy sky at the right. The day of the month, "5," and the Theseion in the middle of the composition suggest the possibility that this drawing was made only a few hours later than the daylight scene of "Athens 5.6. June" described just above. But Lear was in Athens at least twice more during the course of this, his first, tour in Greece, so it would not be wise to be dogmatic on this point. Altogether it is a strange, somber drawing; but it may be deeper in color now than was originally intended, through a darkening of the cream-colored paper on which it was executed because of too great exposure to light in the years since it was completed.

One of the loveliest of all the Lear "Greece" drawings at Harvard (it should be noted that there are many more "Greece" drawings in the Gennadius Library at Athens) is the exquisite watercolor (plate 28; 4 1/2 x 14 1/4

inches) of the Acropolis in profile, "Athens 23 July 1848," evidently drawn near sunset. A lemon-yellow light suffuses the sky to the west; the eastern side of the Acropolis is in shadow; all the mountains to the north are blue and gray. The great Corinthian columns of the Olympeion (Temple of Zeus) rear their lonely heads in the right middle ground. All the foreground is covered by open fields. This was one of the hours of the day that Lear liked best. No wonder he has captured its charm and its peace!

"Between Chalcis and Castella June 22. 1848" (plate 29; 8 1/4 x 17 3/4 inches), from the Island of Euboea, reverts to the style of "Melazzo," with its nearly complete absence of life. This drawing is illustrated in color in Lady Strachey's *Later Letters of Edward Lear* (1911) as then belonging to Canon Charles Church, one of Lear's earliest friends. In Lady Strachey's first book of *Letters* (1907), on page 11, is quoted a passage from a letter of Lear to Chichester Fortescue (later Lord Carlingford), which comes close to describing this very subject: "On the 13th (of June) Church and I set out. Chalcis is most interesting & picturesque, what figures! Would, ah, I could draw the figures! We then resolved to do Euboea, so 19th, Eretria, very fine. Aliveri & Kumi. 21st. Pass of mountains grangrongrously magnificent! Alas for the little time to draw! . . . I must stop for I am not much writable yet . . ."

In another quick jump, we move across the Aegean

Sea to the shores of the Bosphorus and to the "Sweet Waters of Asia" (plate 30; 10 x 18 1/4 inches). By "September 1st, 1848," the date of this drawing, Lear was in Constantinople, where he suddenly — and only temporarily — seems to have been struck by the bright colors of the East. This is a rich, clear-colored drawing, with a heavy sky and many Turkish figures, clad in red, blue, green, and violet robes. Two small watercolors are brighter still, with deep blue sea and sky. Signed and dated simply "1848," one of them, called "Constantinople" (plate 31a; 3 1/2 x 6 1/2 inches) shows two of the great mosques on the Golden Horn; the other, "Beybek (Beylerbey), Bosphorus," (plate 31b; 3 1/2 x 6 1/2 inches) shows the palace in which Sultan Abdul Hamid II was to spend his last days, not far from the plain of the "Sweet Waters of Asia." And finally, from this part of Turkey, "Gallipoli 10 Sept. 1848" (plate 32; 6 3/4 x 10 inches) features the dock where the steamer for Saloniki used to depart and land in that small city on the strait of the Dardanelles. This rather elaborate wash drawing — it is more that than a watercolor — is one of Lear's few (partial) seascapes. For Lear rather feared the sea and hardly ever showed it except in a flat calm, as it is here. Surely this reveals again how much Lear's emotions affected his choice of subjects, the times of day that he depicted them, and indeed the whole general character of his work.

We now come to a series of four fine large softly colored landscape drawings that Lear next made, after he had taken the steamer from Gallipoli to Saloniki and had started up into Macedonia on horseback, accompanied by Giorgio, his servant. His view of "Ostrovo 15 Sept. 1848" (plate 33; 12 3/4 x 20 3/4 inches), shows a town that is already two hard days' ride from Saloniki, which demonstrates how quickly Lear had moved since leaving Saloniki early on the 13th. This exact scene is described in Lear's *Journal of a Landscape Painter in Albania* (1851), on pages 43 and 44: "The drenching tempest ceased at half-past one, and I found myself looking down on the Lake of Ostrovo, whose dark gray bosom stretched dimly into worlds of clouded heights on either side of its extent . . . the little town and mosque shone out brightly against the lead-coloured waters and cloud-swept mountains, a scene of grandeur." Here one finds Lear's drawing exactly matches his words — a feat not many artists or authors are able to accomplish.

"Akhrida" (Ochrid, now in Yugoslav Macedonia but then still Turkish), "23 Sept. 1848" (plate 34; 13 1/4 x 20 3/4 inches), is about as handsome and complicated a pen-and-wash topographical drawing as Lear ever made, with the same somber ocher, violet, and gray coloring. Once again the Albanian *Journal* can be quoted (page 76): "Certainly Akhrida is a beautiful place. All the hillside below the fortress is thickly studded with Mohammedan tombs . . . From the streets below parties of women . . . take the air, and near me several crimson and purple coated Gheges [local townspeople] smoke abstractedly on scattered bits of rock."

"Berat [now in Albania]. October (14) 1848" (plate 36; 20 3/4 x 14 1/4 inches) is perhaps the most surprising drawing of the group, because it actually shows more people than scenery, all in natural attitudes. Here there is real progress in figure drawing. Why did Lear not draw figures more frequently? We can only conclude he did not care to; for this is an accomplished study, with figures in no less than six planes before the drawing of the town is reached. A slightly different drawing from another angle is reproduced in the *Journal* opposite page 188, from which the following passage is quoted: "I was at once struck by the entire change of costume in this district — that of the Tóskhides. Instead of the purple frock, scarlet vest, black waistcoat, and short kilt of Ghegeria, here all is white . . . Beyond the bazaars . . . is a wide open space by the river, whence the view of the dark gorge of the Beratíno, the town and castle are truly wondrous. On one side of this piazza or marketplace is a large new khan, and here I took possession of a corner room looking out on to the busy scene that extends to the foot of the hill — a space in which hundreds of figures sat continually before me for their pictures without suspicion or restraint."

The next to last of this Balkan series for which there is space in a survey of Lear's whole landscape-drawing career is labeled "Apollonia 19 October 1848" (plate 37; 12 1/4 x 20 3/4 inches). It has no number in Lear's hand, as all the other three Macedonian drawings have, but it is certain that it is about the one hundred and sixteenth that Lear had made since he left Saloniki at seven o'clock on the morning of September 13. That is an average of nearly five large drawings a day, which — considering the difficulties and speed of his travel, for by now he was well into present-day Albania near the Adriatic coast — is a notable achievement. On this drawing, too, the *Journal* (pages 209–210) is specific: "In spite of all those superfluous goats . . . not a drop of milk is to be had; but this I have long observed to be a general rule in Italy as well as in Greece. The more goats the less milk . . . Taking a peasant from the convent as a guide, I went at sunrise to the single Doric column — the only remaining token of Apollonia above ground . . . On every side of this single relic of grandeur, how noble are the [mountains] in the distance."

One final Macedonian drawing deserves to be mentioned because it is much smaller in size and on thin gray, rather than on heavy white, paper. It is labeled "Monastir 19 Sept. 1848" (plate 35; 8 1/4 x 11 1/2 inches). That it was probably executed on this trip is evidenced by the date and the number of the drawing (35), yet it is different enough to cause one to wonder whether Lear carried several different pads of paper or might have made this drawing *later* than the date, perhaps after he returned home. Only one other drawing of the hundred-and-fifty-odd "Albanian" drawings at Harvard resembles it, and it is exceedingly close to the one illustrated in the *Journal* opposite page 52. Could Lear have sent the original of that (which Harvard does not have and therefore is not illustrated) and made this as a copy for his files? Yet it is as sharp, incisive, and strong a "penned out" watercolor-washed drawing as any of the preceding ones. Against the theory that this is a copy is the fact that it has many pen notes for color, texture, etc. Why should Lear have inserted them in a copy that he had already colored? And *pencil* notes are to be seen below the pen ones. One comes to the conclusion that Lear *did* have several varieties of drawing paper with him on this expedition.

Still another jump now: to Egypt where Lear spent most of the winter of 1848. "Cairo 10 January 1849" (plate 38; 12 1/4 x 19 3/4 inches) faces the city from the south and on the Gizeh side of the Nile, looking directly at the Citadel and its Mosque of Mohammed Ali. More noteworthy artistically is "Sinai 27 January 1849 4 p.m." (plate 40; 12 1/2 x 19 1/2 inches) — only barely "penned out," with rudimentary washes of ocher, gray, and a band of Chinese white in the sky — and it proves that Lear had continued far on his travels with but little rest. The monastery of St. Catherine's on Mount Sinai is a very long hard trip from Cairo, even by automobile. What it was in 1849 by camel — and muleback the reader can be left to imagine!

By the middle of March, nevertheless, Lear was back in Greece, riding over equally difficult roads in the Peloponnesus. "Leondari & Sparta 22 March 1849 3 pm" (plate 42; 10 x 14 1/2 inches) is the sixty-first drawing in a new series, and "Nemea 31 March 1849" (plate 43; 7 x 10 1/2 inches) is the hundred and third. Significant details about each of these drawings should be mentioned. The "Sparta" drawing gives the time of day as few drawings had done previously (although "Sinai" did). "Nemea," on the other hand, is almost pure shorthand. Very few of Lear's first "positioning" sketches were penned out and kept as this one was, yet we cannot doubt that a first impression was often recorded as we have noted in the margins of certain drawings made during 1844 and '45. Because "Nemea" is so rapid — almost abstract — it is a drawing that modern art critics may like. Unfortunately, not many other such shorthand sketches have survived — except the nonsense drawings, which were exactly of this type with a lot of added humorous sophistication.

Lear made at least one very handsome drawing of Delphi "on the 16th April 1849 1 pm," but it offers nothing unusual, whereas "Parga 7 May, 1849 7 pm" (plate 44; 9 x 14 1/2 inches), made on the Ionian coast of Greece, is on the same rare gray paper as the "Monastir" (plate 35), and is roughly the same size. "Parga" has additional attractions which should be noted. First, it returns to the brown wash technique of the 1844–45 drawings, and, second, it has one of Lear's (heartfelt, no doubt) touches of humor. Penned carefully into the lower right hand corner of the drawing are the words "O fleas of Splantza!"

An even more poignant series of "inscriptions" was soon to come. On "18 May 1849 7 pm" Lear was evidently working in the Vale of Tempe near Mount Olympus: his drawing is labeled "Baba (Tempe)" (plate 45; 10 3/4 x 17 inches). Apparently here nostalgia overcame him: "O! little Girgenti," "owl! (gufo)," "Pipe, pipe pipe!" are among the many asides he has noted on this drawing. It shows two fishermen sitting on the river bank, looking at a fish nearly as large as they are swimming upright in the river like a mermaid! Lear's nationalistic general observation on the whole scene is: "A sort of quiet Arundel old millpond!" So much digression was unusual with Lear, however; he usually sharply differentiated between his hours of work and his moments of play.

He added no quaint comments to his wash drawing of "Olympus from Larissa May 21, 1849" (plate 49; 11 x 20 1/2 inches) being too much impressed, no doubt, with the mountain's majesty. Years later, in 1885, he used this scene as the basis for an illustration (No. 15) to his friend Tennyson's *Poems*, with the legend: "The purple mountain yonder . . . Olympus (Thessaly)." And this respect for a particular scene is characteristic of nearly all the drawings Lear loved best. At Janina (Epirus) on May 29 he was led to comment "horrid scraping Turkish music" on his largest drawing; but by the next autumn, when he returned to Albania, he was serious again. "Scutari 4 October 1849" (plate 46; 7 x 20 3/4 inches) is a particularly effective drawing with a good deal of atmosphere in the rain clouds above the fortress and the lake, whereas a sketch of Thermopylae (plate 47; 5 3/4 x 18 inches) made perhaps six months later is as calm and quietly washed in pale grays and blues as ever. In a word, Lear did not change the general style of his drawings much in the years 1847–1849. He simply varied them.

Having become tired of the hardships of travel in Albania, Epirus, Thessaly, and other remoter parts of northern Greece, he decided to return to England to digest all the experiences he had had and to see his friends again. From the end of 1849 to 1853 he lived in England — a reason, perhaps, why there seem to be few drawings from this period; there are none at all in the large collection at Harvard. When he was in England, Lear was usually unproductive. He evidently needed the color of the Mediterranean and the incentive of remote parts of foreign lands to inspire him to draw. His busy social life in London, and the cold English climate, which seriously affected his health and spirits, are other reasons.

Maturity: Second Period, 1853–1873

Late in 1853, Lear once more felt an irresistible desire to travel. So he went again to Egypt in order to escape from the rigors of another English winter. In Cairo, on or about December 23, he met Richard Burton, the adventurer and explorer, just back from a pilgrimage to

Mecca, which he had succeeded in reaching disguised as an Arab. This trip was destined to make Burton famous. Lear was impressed with his dress, and his huge, brooding dark eyes, and drew him twice. These drawings of Burton are among the very few portrait drawings by Lear in the whole Harvard collection. Because of this fact, and because one of the richly watercolored drawings has a bit of landscape in the background, there seems a justification for its inclusion here (plate 50a; 9 x 6 inches). By the 29th of December, however, Lear had dropped Burton, who was always difficult to get along with, and portraiture as well. Instead, he was out sketching on the edge of the Nile, entranced by the sails of the "fellukahs," the distant view of the pyramids, and the sunset. His drawing (plate 50b; 5 3/4 x 9 inches) is so discreet in color and draughtsmanship that it may be considered one of the few successful renderings of this difficult subject the artist ever made.

On "February 7th, 4 1/2 pm," Lear was at Assouan, drawing the swirling waters of the First Cataract (plate 51; 13 x 19 3/4 inches) and succeeding in making a better drawing of rough water, aided by the later "penning out" and quick pastel washes, than one would have ever expected. On the "10 of February" he reached Kôm Ombo, still buried in yellow sand (plate 52; 12 1/4 x 19 3/4 inches). It was, indeed, mainly "sand & mud brix," according to his penciled notations, but there were some "hawx" (flying about, one supposes — they are not shown) and the stones, he felt, were "just like those below Winchelsea & Hastings." On "February 12th 5 pm" he was drawing "Edfoo" (Idfu) in a near sunset glow (plate 53; 11 1/4 x 19 3/4 inches). He was not successful with the camels he placed in the left foreground, so we should perhaps be pleased he did not attempt the "mangy pigeons" that he noted should "always be inserted." He also sadly added: "I can't wait for the effect" — of the full sunset — but he noted that all the lower part of the town was "blue from mist or smoke." This effect he admirably achieved by his middle ground washes of blue-gray and purple in his "penning out." The "Edfoo" drawing was the two-hundredth made on this expedition.

Here in Lear's "mature" landscape career one must skip ahead rather more rapidly to avoid repetition of subjects and types of drawing already discussed and reproduced, for he repeated a great deal. He loved to go back to very nearly the same spot that he had drawn from before, if he liked it particularly, and then to make a new drawing with a few small details changed but little new added to the old. If this habit is revealed in the over three thousand four hundred landscape drawings at Harvard, how much more it would appear to be true if all the "ten thousand" drawings he is reported to have left could be found and placed together! On "18 Sept. 1856," for example, back in Greece, he did a fine large splashy drawing of "Athos," a mountain he loved and drew or painted from almost the same angle again and again over a period of years (plate 54; 13 1/2 x 21 inches). Clearly the time is always "near sunrise" or sunset (by preference), so that the lofty bare rocky peak can glow with pink — or with blazing yellow and white in winter. The trees in the foreground are nearly always dark blue and green, and the sky as usual is nearly always clear. In the drawing of Mount Athos shown in plate 54 there is no person in the foreground but there is a tiny trial pen sketch on the right. For this was Lear's first visit to the famous peninsula and in two months there he was as greatly excited by the views as he was depressed by the monasteries. Unluckily the food was also bad, and he caught a prevailing fever. No one who has read his letters to Chichester Fortescue on the subject (Lady Strachey's *Letters*, page 41, or Angus Davidson's biography, pages 100–101) can forget its climax, the anathema he expressed the desire to hurl after the monastic brothers: "these muttering, miserable mutton-hating, man-avoiding, misogynic, morose and merriment marring, monotoning, many-mule-making, mocking, mournful, minced-fish and marmalade masticating Monx!"

Fifty drawings in all, apparently, were made during this trip to the Holy Mountain, Lear's illness notwithstanding. Then he returned by way of the Aegean Islands to Corfu, where he lived from 1855 to 1858. In addition to drawings of the town and its citadel, there is a very fine drawing dated "12 December 1856" at Palaeocastritza ("old castle"), which actually lies above the tiny port of the same name, with many figures in the foreground lightly sketched and washed in with color (plate 55; 13 1/4 x 20 3/4 inches).

A serious problem of dating Lear's "penned out" drawings now arises. In the section dealing with Lear's technical procedure it has been noted that his "penning out" usually took place not very long after his original sketch was made on the spot. Now a drawing of "Zante" in the writer's possession at Harvard (reproduced as the frontispiece of this book) bears two dates nine years apart! The first, 1848, is doubtless when the original sketch was made, on Lear's first trip to the Ionian Islands, for it is next to the word "Zante" towards the lower left of the drawing. But then Lear took the trouble, in the case of this highly colored and finished drawing, to sign again at the very bottom (left): "Edward Lear del. 1857." Surely, this would indicate by the letters "del." for "delineavit," that he drew (that is, "penned out") the drawing all these years later when (very possibly) he sold it to a client. A client would want the drawing to be "up to date" perhaps! In any case, he would care more about the dating than Lear would when he worked for himself alone. It is, therefore, necessary to watch closely for changes in style of washes or of "penning out" in dating the later Lear drawings.

Many of the W.B.O. Field drawings at Harvard, being

from Lear's bequest to Lushington, were the artist's reference drawings; the drawings he made for sale to his clients have emerged mainly in more recent years, as prices have been rising. Lear rarely signed the early drawings that he intended to keep for his own reference; he only dated them, and added the hour as an indication of the light and shadows. But from 1857 on we begin to see his initials — a capital "E" within the loop of a larger capital script "L" — fairly frequently; or, as is the case in the Zante drawing, his whole name carefully written out.

Another example comes to hand easily, also in the writer's possession. Entitled simply "Petra 1858" (plate 57; 9 3/4 x 15 1/4 inches), it has this "E.L." device just beneath the place name, and is fully "penned out" and elaborately colored, although in a rather different, slightly looser style than the colored drawing of Zante. This is, actually, so close to the painting of Petra reproduced opposite page 112 of Davidson's biography that one might say they were done at the same time if only this drawing at Harvard did not happen to have four figures instead of none in the left foreground! Of course, one cannot judge of the color in the painting reproduced in Davidson's biography because the reproduction is in black and white, but the technique in plate 57 is slightly broader, with no exact articulation of the tree forms such as is to be seen in the Davidson reproduction (plate 109; 36 x 60 inches).

Lear was obviously filled with wonder when he came upon this view of Petra. The then only recently rediscovered city of the Nabataeans (in the present Jordan) was even more beautiful than he had expected. Lear's journal (as quoted by Sir Franklin Lushington in *Macmillan's Magazine* for April 1897) describes it all with delight. And Giorgio, his servant ("prone to culinary similes," as Davidson wryly observes) exclaimed, "Oh, master we have come into a world where everything is made of chocolate, ham, curry-powder, and salmon." Giorgio's words nearly describe the original drawing at Harvard in every respect, except its dark greens and dark blues. Unfortunately, the pages in the first of Lear's manuscript diaries at Harvard, which should have an account of his trip to Petra, are blank. It is only through the journal (present whereabouts unknown to me) quoted by Lushington that we have Lear's account of coming upon this view, of being robbed by bandits, but of enjoying himself no end — at least in retrospect — as all good travelers do.

On this same trip, in the spring of 1858, Lear visited Jerusalem, where he made some beautifully detailed drawings both outside and inside the city, dated May 4 and later. If only in the second of the two drawings reproduced (plates 58 and 59; 7 x 20 and 6 1/2 x 20 inches, respectively) he had included the "roziz in potz on roof" that he called for in his penciled notes on the drawing! But Lear's humor was capricious. By the time he came to "penning out," he exactly transcribed his penciled directions, but failed to draw the roses in. No doubt he was tired by then — and the "roziz" could always be added later if the drawing were to be sold, or an oil made. At Baalbek, on May 23, he noted on one of his drawings the contrast between the yellowed marble and stone and the "sno-sno-sno" on the great Lebanon mountain range which rises to eleven thousand feet in the background. Evidently "Hoopoes" and "Kestrils" flew about in the ruins, as he sat on the enormous fallen "blox." And although his best drawing (plate 60; 7 1/2 x 21 3/4 inches) — number 209 since he started this sketching trip at Alexandria on March 17 — was done probably at some other time of day, Lear wrote in pencil "make it sunset." So sunset it is, after being "penned out," with a purple light along the whole range of the mountains. A note of sadness suits Baalbek, and Lear's mood that day, as so often, was very sad.

In 1862, Lear was once again living on the island of Corfu, continually sketching the town and its citadel from near and from far. One of his favorite far view-points was just off the Benitza road, near Gasturi (plate 61; 6 1/2 x 10 1/4 inches). A view so close to this as to be almost identical is lithograph No. 4 in Lear's *Views in the Seven Ionian Islands* (London, 1863), about which he comments in the text: "This is one of the loveliest views in the Island, and is distant about six miles from the City. The beautiful slopes of olive-wood seem to end in the church-crowned Promontory of Ascension, but

this is not the case . . . the Citadel, the town of Corfu, Vido . . . the Santa Quaranta hills, and those of Butrinto, are all beyond . . . The landscape is finished by many-pointed Mount Lykursi, the Pass of Gardiki, and the long chain of heights . . ." Probably Lear made the first sketch for this very highly finished watercolor on April 5, 1862 (it is signed "E.L. 1862"), since in his diary for that day he says: "Very calm, warm, fine, windless all day . . . worked at Gasturi view . . ." No other entry comes so close to the scene as it is here reproduced, in the light of the late afternoon.

A few hours later he may have drawn a near view of the citadel, in the Harvard collection. For, by this time, he had come close to home, and the citadel was no longer in the slanting light of the setting sun. Twilight had begun; the sea was like a mill pond. These two drawings are almost exactly of the same size and degree of finish, but the second one is not dated. Another drawing, owned by the writer, is from the same close point of view, and at the same time of day. Only the boats in the foreground have changed. This was one of Lear's most characteristic habits, to vary his scenes by the incidental figures or objects. Otherwise, they remained very similar — again and again. See, for example, plate 108 (a: 5 1/2 x 9 1/4, b: 2 1/2 x 3 1/2, c: 4 1/2 x 7 1/8 inches).

Soon Lear moved out once more to Palaeocastritza, where he wrote a charming note in his diary for Easter Sunday, April 20, 1862: "wonderfully lovely all day . . .

How glorious was the blue level of sea! . . . Sabia & the white butterflies — a quiet of bygone days . . . Abruzzi & 1843. Do you ever think of Donna —? I hope not. Yet your lot in those few bright days was better than it ever had been & I fear ever could be. And you — of Castella days? Where are you and your babe —? A dream world . . ." How poignantly sad! His diary entry ended: "Palaeocastritza memories, if I live, will live with me." But on April 21, the very next day, he wrote: "Did not sleep well . . . Rose however at 5:40 & at 6:30 drew one more view . . . returning at 4 to draw the rock scene — wh. took me to 5:40 — when I was 'utterly outworn'. Palaeocastritza [in Greek letters], beautiful as it is, wearies me — [it is] only a mass of foregrounds after the first general views are taken: then it is so devoted to [great] swells, — and so un-country like in its ways, though so untownlike in its position. So I go! — And leave Duhades & Lacones, to other times. If indeed such times come — for I truly weary of Corfu . . . I would fain see the East once more: just now . . . I am covered with fleas & sad." Thus changeable were all Lear's moods from the moment he began the diary of 1858 to the end of his life.

At Harvard there is a drawing dated on that same Easter Sunday, 1862, that is brightly colored, with a particularly dark blue sea, made from a place on the sand near the water in front of what is now the little Hotel Zephyr on the tiny port. This fits in perfectly with Lear's diary entry for that day. But he made several better drawings from this port later, especially a remarkable highly finished drawing labeled "Palaeocastritza, Corfu E.L. 1863" (plate 62; 13 1/2 x 22 3/4 inches), which is "penned out" by brush in black and white because it probably is the drawing for lithograph No. 6 in Lear's *Ionian Islands* folio (also there in monochrome), which seems to be identical except for a number of small details. The angle of view and the figures in the foreground are the same, but there is no fisherman on the rocks at the left in the lithograph, the skyline varies slightly, the position of the initials have changed, and there is no date. The scene, however, must have been drawn in the spring of 1863, when Lear made a final tour of the Ionian Islands to finish the drawings for his book before returning to England so that the book could be published on December first.

In 1864, the artist's most exciting new venture was a trip to the island of Crete, where "Suda Bay, Canea" was drawn on April 15 (plate 63; 14 x 23 1/4 inches). Once again Lear was happy, as witness his diary entry: "Then went on — across [on the isthmus] to the wondrous Suda Bay view, where [Mount] Ida — if indeed it be Ida — was clear & splendid, tho' all the rest was purple cold. Drew till 12:30 & then went to rocks opposite the end of Suda Bay . . . where I lunched on eggs, oranges and wine." Nothing could represent this description more clearly than the drawing in question, although he has inadvertently changed the "purple" cold to "blue," in accordance with his own written instructions on the drawing itself: "Ida bright W. [white] against gray pale, rest of the range *blue*." This drawing is among the largest and finest at Harvard.

Later that year, Lear attempted one of his rare views of an agitated sea. The view is from some great rocks on the Italian Riviera where Lear took a walking trip from Nice to Genoa and back. And once again Lear altered his colors. In the drawing the sea is blue. In the diary he wrote: ". . . the rolling green sea was magnificent, [through] a tunnel & drew Finale, very picturesque, till dark. Town by 5." This represents, in words, "Finale 4:15 pm 16 Decbr 1864" (plate 64; 14 1/4 x 23 inches), which Lear copied once in pen about 1874 and then, again, to create a gray and black wash drawing (No. 164) for Tennyson's *Poems* in 1885 (plate 65; 5 x 7 3/4 inches).

Late in 1865, Lear went to the island of Malta, where he wrote ecstatically in his diary: "Today again has been wholly celestial. Cloudless sunrise — air like early summer English morning — the brightness & loveliness was a real delight . . . watching the wonderful sunrise I then *painted* violently . . ." Ah, here is a new word! Does Lear mean *sketched* or really painted (in watercolor or oil)? The drawing at Harvard, "Sliema, Malta 30 December 1865" (plate 66; 8 1/4 x 22 inches), *is* brushed in with watercolor. Could Lear have varied his

constant habit and "painted" with watercolors in the open air? One is not sure, Lear being the creature of impulse that he was. We can be certain, however, that a beautiful weird night scene also at Sliema on Malta (plate 67; 7 3/4 x 14 1/2 inches), was not "penned out" on the spot, because it is dated March 1, 1866, when according to his diary "the moon was hid by clouds." It was on the night before (February 28) that he wrote in his diary: "The still moonlight is wonderful! Dined — penned (out) & wrote . . ." The "penning out" of the moonlight sketch must have taken place the next day.

We move now to April 1866 and the Bay of Cattaro (now Kotor, Yugoslavia), where Lear seems again to have been happy. He drew the town with its picturesque walls and the twisting road leading up to Cetinje in Montenegro at least four times from the same spot across the bay. The first drawing at Harvard is labeled "Cattaro 6:30 pm 26 April 1866"; the mountain is noted as "gold." Two others are labeled "Cattaro — 7 pm 29 April 1866"; in one of these (plate 68; 7 x 10 1/2 inches) the color indication has been changed (because it is a half hour later in time) to "gold gray." This drawing may be the preliminary sketch for the writer's highly finished watercolor with figures and boats in the foreground (plate 69; 6 1/2 x 10 1/4 inches), which has no date, but simply the familiar cypher "E.L." that Lear used mainly on works that he sold. Lear has even given this intricate drawing, as detailed as any of his paintings, a steamboat (left foreground) and much shipping in the port (far right). But his diary entry for April 29 is disappointing — and even misleading: ". . . after 5:30 or 6 — walk to the other side — trying to draw — but it grows too dark. The hedges are of pomegranate. Return after 7:30, & take some food . . ." This finished drawing must have been penned out and colored later, yet it is one of his nicest small drawings because it has some atmosphere as well as mood.

The next jump in our account is to January 6, 1867, when Lear was once more in Egypt — his wish "to go to the East again" expressed at Corfu in 1863 satisfied after four long years. Yet immediately he became miserable. In his diary he wrote: "Suffered horribly from toothache" (and then he inserted the X which as has been said probably indicates a slight epileptic attack). "At 7 a.m. find the wind became N for a short time . . . Walk a bit and draw a bit by a sugar plantation 'wherein,' says A (Lear's dragoman), 'one pig, big two time dog!' When sugar he be cut, pig he go [to the] desert" (plate 70; 5 1/2 x 9 inches).

Lear, like the pig when the sugar was cut, went intrepidly on — all the way to Abou Simbel on the edge of the Sudan, where he drew his 376th sketch of this trip, high up on a sand bank, level with one of the great heads of Rameses II. The time was "1:30 pm 8 Feby 1867" (plate 71; 9 3/4 x 13 3/4 inches). But before that, this is the way his diary starts the day: "O sleeplessness! o bumps! o nerves! o stomach! (x 2) But I woke at 5:30 . . . " Then at last his spirits rose: "[As we] approach the low sandy cliffs, the sailors' songs echo back from the high eastern rocks . . . [then] in turning the corner [of the river] forth suddenly came the Rameses Heads!! I was absolutely too astonished & affected to draw, so I lost my sketch, and must go back for it . . . [Finally] I drew several times above where the vast statues combine with the distant Nile & dark purple hills . . . As a whole the scene is overpowering from its beauty — color — solitude — history — art — poetry — every sort of association . . ."

Egypt explored to its southern limits, we come now to the only other important trip Lear took before the great voyage to India and Ceylon: his journey to Corsica, described in the last of his travel books, *Journal of a Landscape Painter in Corsica* (London, 1870). The trip took place in 1868, and resulted in a very large number of drawings. Many, for a change, were rather small in size. Large views like the scene of rocky peaks and pine woods (Forest of Bavella, near the top of a pass called the Bocca di Larone) shown in plate 72 (11 1/2 x 18 inches), are also more numerous than ever; Harvard has over three hundred. And here Lear seems to have followed a new procedure. The illustrations in his Corsican *Journal* are not lithographs made entirely by himself, as in his previous books, but wood engravings cut by various professional craftsmen from Lear's designs on the wood blocks. The names of these men are all French, except for what would appear to be one Englishman, J. D. Cooper.

Lear thanks them in a note at the end of the Preface to the *Journal;* he should rather have complained, for the engravings are poor. And reducing his drawings must have taken a lot of Lear's time, after which he still had to transfer, or to draw, the designs on to the wood blocks. Harvard has a reduced copy of the "Forest of Bavella" drawing, in colors, but unsigned (plate 95; 4 3/4 x 7 5/8 inches); it is exactly the size of the wood engraving (by Badoureau) in the book, opposite page 92. Some figures have been inserted in the right foreground to lend scale. Lear signed his drawing on the wood block with his cypher and further developed the four figures, so the Harvard drawing, evidently, was not transferred. (It is on very heavy paper, and is in the same direction as the print.) In the engraving for the book, M. Badoureau made a hash of the right hillside, causing it to seem completely forested, when in fact the uplands, according to Lear's two color drawings, are mainly fields and stone. One could cite many other instances of the engravers' mistakes.

There are some other small Corsican drawings at Harvard which belong to the writer. These have been reduced from large originals, and are executed in a different technique. They are worked pencil drawings, with touches of "penning out," and with not over two or three very simple washes — ocher, black, and gray — like the views representing the town of Calvi seen from near by (plate 73a; 4 3/4 x 7 1/2 inches) and Grosseto seen from afar (plate 73b; 5 x 7 3/4 inches). This, as we have seen in the case of the town of Corfu, was a favorite device of Lear's; when he was particularly struck by a prominent landmark, he made drawings from various points of view. Lear drew two Calvi sketches on or about May 29th, 1868, according to the *Journal* (page 222). The near view (plate 73a), is reproduced almost exactly in the wood engraving opposite page 224 in the Corsican *Journal.* The far view is totally different, and is weak, long, and thin. Evidently Lear and his publisher changed their minds about what would best fit in on a page of text.

Lear later had a wonderful time embellishing his own copy of this *Journal* (given by the writer to Harvard). It has pencil sketches here and there throughout the book: doodles, nonsense drawings, some landscapes, and several hideous blobs of india ink on the title page which have transferred over to the frontispiece: a wood engraving of Ajaccio. On the verso of the title Lear has drawn several doodles in pencil, using ink patches already there to achieve a grenadier guard and a man with mustachios. Above them he has scrawled in ink "Two Blots on Corsica! Oh dear, dear, dear, Mr. Edward Lear," followed by a very quick *ferocious* caricature of his cat and then the words, "Foss did it!" These additions were probably made well after 1870 when the *Journal* was published. One even gains the impression from studying them that they may have been done during his last years (after 1875) in San Remo, when he was idle, tired, or ill.

During 1869, Lear went to Paris and to Cannes, where he drew many scenes of the famous French Riviera coast. He also went once more to London. And then he moved at last, in 1871, to San Remo, which was to be his principal abode for the rest of his life. The Franco-Prussian War, which broke out in 1870, thoroughly frightened him; Cannes was too expensive and its wealthy British colony, despite their potential as clients, were "a norful bore." So he finally settled upon San Remo and the "Villa Emily," which his close English friends, with loans and commissions, somehow enabled him to build. Here also he acquired Foss, his cat.

For two years he led a relatively peaceful and uneventful life, as befitted a man of his age who had wandered far and wide for over thirty years. But he was not entirely contented, and the books he planned and the "nonsenses" he wrote rarely satisfied him. Peace was something Lear could never quite find. When early in 1872 Lord Northbrook, an old friend who had just been appointed Viceroy of India, offered to take him out to India for a year, all expenses paid, in return for only a few pictures which Lear was to paint, the offer was deeply gratifying. But at the moment Lear resisted on

account of his new house. It was not until the following year that he became again dangerously tempted to take the greatest and longest trip of his whole life.

Maturity: Third Period, 1873–1875 (*India*)

After Lord Northbrook renewed his offer to Lear in 1873, the decision whether to go or not to go to India in October gave the artist many anxious hours. In the end he went, and made the trip a success by producing two volumes of a manuscript journal and over fifteen hundred drawings (nearly all given by W. B. O. Field to Harvard). Such a figure is exceedingly impressive considering Lear's age, the heat, the risk of disease, and the fact that the trip lasted only a little over a year, until the end of January 1875.

To choose from all Harvard's India drawings is difficult indeed, but certainly two from the sea voyage should be included. The first sketch of the trip seems to have been made going through the Suez Canal, on November 3, 1873, at 2 p.m. From Lear's diary comes the following entry: "G. [Giorgio] awakened me before sunrise, & I got on deck just as we entered the canal — a strange long view of Sandbanx & water! Lots of Flamingoes & other birds . . . Bkft. Nasty Doctor! First ship [that passed] Dutch. 2d French man of war, — soldiers — & lots of Apes . . . 3 pm finished a small sketch" (plate 74; 6 1/4 x 13 3/4 inches). Then nine days later, at 6 p.m., his ship reached Aden at the end of the Red Sea (plate 75; 6 x 13 1/2 inches), where he was cross with Giorgio and repented later; and finally his ship carried him out into the Indian Ocean to a subcontinent and a land totally different from any he had ever seen before. Naturally, therefore, his drawings are rather different, too!

For example, "Darjeeling 8:30–9:30 am 18 Jany 1874" (plate 76; 13 3/4 x 22 3/4 inches) shows a view of Mount Kanchenjunga, which is all snowy white with the exception of light gray-blue washes for the shadows. Lear's diary adds this summary description: "Dressed by 6:15 . . . & we were on the highest point above the Church by 7. The mountains were clear and wondrous — but it was awful cold!!! Yet I drew on till nearly 10 o'clock. Kinchenjunga [sic] is not a Sympathetic Mountain: it is so far off — so very godlike & stupendous — & all those dark opal vallies [sic] of misty, hardly to be conceived of forms."

A few hours later, he drew more conventionally a view of the mountain station (plate 77; 13 3/4 x 20 3/4 inches) as his manuscript journal also relates: "Next we returned for books, etc. — & then, — (often losing my way,) I got to a point whence I drew the station & the hills, which are more or less clear all today. G. went down for Tobacco, & by 3 we started afresh . . . The

people returning from the Bazaars were a sight!" In this pale washed drawing one should notice the "people," and the fact that Lear put a number of his directions in Greek (an old habit that he steadily continued, even when he was no longer in Greece).

A disappointing drawing, which should, nevertheless, be reproduced because the purpose of this book is to show all the ramifications of Lear's landscape draughtsmanship, is "Agra. The Taj . . . 1 to 3 pm 15th & 16th Feby 1874" (plate 78; 13 1/2 x 20 1/2 inches). Here, under February 15, his journal says: "First sight of the Taj — vastly larger than I had expected"; and under February 16, "What a garden! What flowers! What gorgeously dressed and be-ringed women! . . . Men, mostly in white, some with red shawls . . . — the great centre of the Picture being ever the vast glittering Ivory-white Taj, & the accompaniment & contrast of the dark green of the cypresses, with the rich yellow green trees of all sorts! And then the effect of the innumerable flights of bright green Parrots flitting across like live Emeralds; — & of the scarlet leaved Poinsettias & countless other flowers . . . The Tinker or 'tinpot' Bird, ever at work . . . purple flowered Bougainvillea runs up the cypress trees. Aloes also, & some new kind of Fern . . ." Altogether this is a gorgeous verbal description, but either the Taj Mahal itself, or the impossibility of rendering his own words in watercolor washes, has made Lear's drawing seem a rather banal image of one of the greatest sights in the world.

Lear was far more successful with "Roorkee, March 20, 1874 2 to 5 P.M." (plate 79; 13 3/4 x 20 inches), which is intensely "Indian," vivid and powerful in its chartreuse yellow-green and brown-purple washes. The contrast between sunlight and shade is as violent as would be expected in this town of the north plains during the heat of the day in the dry monsoon. The "grove of Mango & Peepul" trees is superb. So, in contrast to the "Taj," this is one of Lear's very best drawings. Lear's journal adds to it: "Sitting by the (Ganges) canal road till 5:30, making 2 drawings of the grand and lovely Mango Grove — very dark pencil sketches & it is to be hoped they will cast the clear brilliancy of those stems! and the intense deep brown of the far hollow arched shades!!" Most interesting for our purposes is Lear's note on the margin of the journal just at this point: "Penned out & colored, September 1876." That was two and a half years later. Lear had been back in San Remo then for more than a year and a half. How remarkable that the drawing is so fresh and immediate!

Equally fine are some of his sketches of Indian landscape details such as the frond of "Poinciana Regia" inscribed "Poonah" on "18 June 1874" (plate 80; 8 1/4 x 13 1/4 inches), and the lotus plants at Sholapur, also near Bombay, "19 July 1874 (plate 81; 8 3/4 x 11 1/4 inches). Of the "Poinciana" he wrote: "Pouring torrents

all night long" (the wet monsoon had arrived); "went out & got a branch of the exquisite Golmohr tree . . . & made drawings of it. Also penned out . . ." Apparently this poinciana drawing was penned out and colored at once. Of the lotuses he wrote: "At noon, set out again to the Mootee Bagh, & drew Lotos plants, getting . . . a lot to take home. Tiffin, cheerful, — but [some Indian drink not decipherable] a mistake, as I am better senza [Italian for "without"]. At 3:30 off in Tonga . . . (horrid carriage!)".

On "June 27th, 1 pm" he finished another of his best Indian drawings, a far-reaching view of the river at Poona (plate 82; 14 1/2 x 21 3/4 inches), and wrote most vividly about it in his journal: ". . . at 12:20 decide to go to the Bundrocks, although there was a high wind, & moreover there was to be a big musicale phunktion in the gardens. Having reached the rocks, difficulties were great. 1stly the wind: so violent that when enough stones were piled on the paper to keep it down, the foglio [folio!] was too heavy to lift — so G. had to hold it hard with both hands while I drew, or tried to draw. 2dly every five minutes, loud cries gave warning of a blasting to be made in the quarries below, so we had to run for it. And 3dly from one of the stones, came a scorpion . . . nearly running down my sleeve [so] that I thought it wiser to let the whole foglio fall to the ground, whereby the paper blew away to all remote quarters of the earth & some was lost for evermore . . . Reached home at 3:30 . . . Penned out again till 6 when I played & sung!! to Major and Mrs. Moray and a slekt ordiance . . . Said George, 'Che Cantava? pareva una prima voce di teatro' . . ." After all this gamut of emotions, work, and wit, Lear finally retired to bed at 9:30. It would seem he was very pleased with himself.

At "Calicut 3 p.m. 21. October 1874 (& 22d Oct.)" Lear made a particularly appealing drawing (plate 83; 13 x 19 1/2 inches). Calicut, now called Kozhikode, is a city far south on the Malabar (west) coast of India. The wet monsoon still prevailed, and Lear was miserable. At such times his diary never fails to reflect his mood to the full: "It poured with rain all night long. Rose at 5:30 . . . went out to try to sketch — but rain came on again, so I came in . . . [Later, went out again and] went through the wonderful palmy road & drew as well as I could — but it is almost impossible to do anything [with] the people about & the constant movement of Oxcarts . . . & the confusion of eye & mind produced by the wonderful vegetation on all sides . . ." And wonderful it was, as can be seen in the drawing. But there is a final twist to Lear's pen, and thoughts, in the lower right-hand corner of the drawing where he wrote, "Oh, ye crows of Malabar, what a cussed bore you are!" Now crows are plentiful on the Malabar coast — all over southern India, in fact, and on the island of Ceylon. But usually they do not gather till near sunset, whereas this watercolored drawing in shades of green, yellow, purple, and brown was made in the middle of the afternoon. Could the "crows" of his verse be an ironic metaphor really meaning "people"? It is very likely, given the entry in his diary quoted above, and his remarks there the next day (October 22): "These Malabar folk stick like burrs or flies — you can't get rid of them."

Shortly thereafter, Lear went to Ceylon on the last leg of his Eastern tour, while the rain still continued. The humidity must have been fearful. From his journal we learn that on Friday, November 27, there was "rain as usual & dismal damp." Nevertheless, Lear managed to breakfast hungrily on "Haddocks, mutton, etc., with five sorts of curries — all good" and "Afterwards, overhauled sketches, & drew till 2!" He could still, on occasion, be an "iron man," if his mood (or health?) was right. On Saturday, November 28, he was "off at 5:45 am" in a carriage from Colombo to Hanwele, where he arrived with Giorgio "at 12:30 pm, and 'drew' from the Duke of Edinburgh's seat. Back to carriage at 12:45. Post Office 3:15. Galle Face Hotel, the filthy, 3:30." A typical hardworking day! But there is one significant fact to note: the drawing (plate 85; 12 3/4 x 19 1/4 inches), penned out and colored later, of course, only took him fifteen minutes, if his journal entry is accurate. And "at dinner . . . the 'proprietor' of this 'Hotel' sate hard by . . . a pig [while] the same Italian boys whom I saw at Jumalpore & elsewhere, played very odious tunes."

Six weeks later, the tour through India and Ceylon

was over. Early in January 1875 Lear returned to Bombay, and on January 11 went aboard the *Sumatra*, bound for home, with "plenty to reflect on concerning the past 13 months & 20 days . . ." Did he realize that this was his last long trip and that his old age had begun? There is no evidence for any such conclusion. Lear's ups and downs proceeded just as usual, aggravated, however, by a severe wrench to his back. Still he continued to rise about five or six each morning during the voyage, and to observe everything, though his manuscript journal entries grew very brief and his diary ceased altogether for a while. But he "drew a little" — and read a lot. For a few days, he planned a book of "Indian Landscapes," but quickly dropped it. On January 27, he reached Brindisi; on January 29, at "7 P.M. Hotel de la Paix. *Sanremo.*" "How strange seems life!" he commented in his journal: "To have come once more to Olive & Lemon trees & all these familiar places after that vast & wonderful India!!" The restful voyage home had cured his back. On the 28th of January, 1875, he recommenced his diary.

Old Age: 1875–1888

The dating of Lear's landscape drawings after 1875 is harder to be precise about, so far as Harvard's holdings are concerned. There are far fewer sketches and more "finished" views. Sometimes it is very difficult to date these last, because Lear copied continually as he traveled less and less. Usually he inserted only the year of the copy, more rarely the date of the original — as if he were slightly embarrassed to confess how long before that had been. Occasionally, he did not bother with a date at all, and one must make a guess based on the technical means used, or on the juxtaposition to dated drawings in his albums, or on the gradual dwindling of fine detail as his eyesight rather rapidly weakened.

At first, of course, there was little change, although his sketches tended to become smaller and his colors more noticeably subdued. He still rose early each day — the habit of a lifetime — in order to profit from the quiet and the morning light, but he dined out less and went to bed earlier. Therefore we are not surprised that he had risen at five as usual before he made a drawing on Lake Lugano, the 17th of August, 1878 (plate 86; 6 1/2 x 11 inches), or that he "got off with G. by 8–8:25 rail to Melide," where he at once "set off to walk & draw . . . the calmness of the Lake truly lovely." What is noteworthy is an increasing tendency to render utter calm in a drawing by many long, nearly vertical, parallel lines placed very close together. In this particular landscape Lear is as careful as ever, but his color is still simpler — only an over-all blue-gray wash for both mountains and lake, varying in shade from one to the other by subtle degrees.

Three days later, in a view of Lake Como from the terrace of the Villa Serbelloni (plate 87; 6 1/2 x 11 inches), his use of gray wash has diminished even further, but the trees are still as extravagantly drawn as they were in India, only on a smaller scale. That day, too, he rose at five, and was off on a "steamer by 8:15 . . . Bellagio by 10:30 . . . omnibus up to V. Serbelloni (where the gardens are) wonderfully interesting for distant views & foliage . . . but the Church bells & clocks are no guide . . . as to time, since they alter the hour according as the steamers arrive early or late."

A year later we find Lear sometimes drawing in quite a different style and vein, more nearly as he did in some of the last Indian drawings but without the use of color. For example, "Monte Generoso. 5:30 pm. August 14, 1879" (plate 92; 12 x 10 1/2 inches) is a detailed pen sketch with practically no color at all, although Lear records that he then enjoyed "perfect weather . . . [in] green meadows beyond the Mandora . . . drew some trees."

The rest of the day, Lear's diary tells us, was spent "at the A.T. subjects"; he had started to work in earnest on illustrations for his friend Tennyson's poems. At this time, he apparently had no very clear idea of how he should do them, except that they should be smaller and more finished than the usual sketches he had been making from nature. "All the outer frame-lines," he records, were now "finished — & 2 of the narrow size penned out — as far as I mean the penning of this new lot to go." What "lot" he refers to is a question, for he gives no particulars or means of identification. This frustrating habit continues over the next seven years of his diary. Again and again he mentions that he is working on Tennyson drawings, or "working them over." Sometimes he gives brief titles, but more often only how many he has done. From the titles, and from the fact that he no longer traveled far, it is clear that he was copying other drawings made during his many trips in the past, probably on a smaller scale, more suitable for book illustrations.

Harvard has a group of such assorted subjects; one is reproduced as plate 65. They are all roughly the same size (5 x 7 1/2 inches), and all oblong. Some are colored, but they are mostly black and white. They were preserved in an album that evidently belonged to the artist, since it has press notices about him, two of which are dated 1887 (within his own lifetime). Since none of these drawings is dated, we are thrown back on surmise, but they are in the style of his late drawings, and often seem to have been cut down in order to "match" one another. Are these (of about 1878–1883) his earliest drawings for the Tennyson subjects? Perhaps, however, the earliest belong to another group of colored drawings, such as the two measuring 4 x 8 3/4 inches, shown in plates 88 and 89. On the first of these the artist has inscribed, at the left, "Athens. Edward Lear 12 June 1848," while on the right, just opposite, he has placed his cypher and the date 1882.

The fact that the drawings of both these groups are of scattered places further suggests that they were part of the Tennyson project, since previously all Lear's books had been composed of drawings made on one or another particular tour and mainly in one country or province. In the drawings under discussion he roams far and wide, as if to show the breadth of his travels. The style in these groups is looser than in any earlier drawings, the outlines usually are less sharp, despite the smaller scale. There is a new and growing feeling for atmospheric effect, not always intentional perhaps, but if not, then due to an inability to show the exact topographical details in such small space, or to a failing memory of them. When there is atmosphere that is intentional one can sense it, as when clouds are shown, and rough seas, or when sunsets (notably in the Athens 1882 drawing, plate 88) are indicated not only by pink bands of clouds, but by an over-all suffused pink, purple, and yellow light.

Lear became increasingly fond of drawing in the early morning and in the evening, because it is then that the weather is apt to be at its most tranquil, and crowds and traffic are at the minimum. So "Muttra [India] Edward Lear. 4 March 1874" (plate 89; 4 x 8 1/2 inches) is drawn soon after sunrise, to match the "Athens" sunset. Again there is the telltale "E.L. 1882" in the opposite corner of the drawing, and there is an equal effort for cloud effects, but the colors are soft yellow, brown, purple, green, and blue instead of the warmer sunset shades. Lear was not disturbed that his scenes were so far apart and related only remotely to Tennyson's poems. He apparently fancied them that way — believing, no doubt, that they complemented the Poet Laureate's wide range of talent and emotion just as they reflected his own wide view of the world.

Once in a while, of course, Lear drew new landscapes on a large scale (not for the Tennyson poems) — views of those parts of Italy and Switzerland that he still visited in the summer months. "Assisi 10 A.M. — 10:45 6 Sept. 1883" (plate 90), is an example. A strong, quick drawing this, "penned out" boldly, with barely a film of light blue wash over most of the foreground — trees and land, not sky! Lear's diary says it was a cloudy day, so the weather cannot account for a coloring that seems to bear no relation to the facts, or to the sky itself, which shows clouds but is not overcast. The emphasis is, of course, on the great Church of San Francesco, with the individual houses more and more roughly blocked out the further they recede from that center of focal interest. This is a big drawing (12 1/2 x 19 1/2 inches), comparable to most of the large ones of earlier days but not nearly so highly finished in details. Nor is another, more distant, view of Assisi from the "Fiume Biaggio. Ponte Bastiolo 12:15 pm" (plate 91; 11 x 19 1/4 inches), made a few hours later on the same day. Its outlines are more rapidly sketched, and the trees are barely indicated. In contrast, the clouds are rather carefully drawn; this, as we have noticed, is something of a new habit, as is the long parallel pen-stroke shading to indicate shadows in the water. But the personal notes on the face of the drawing have their familiar, slightly nonsensical ring: "banx"; "grabble"; "water should be"; and the color on the mountains — were there any — Lear destined to be "all gray squash."

A drawing Lear made a few days earlier at "Abetone 9 9:30 a.m. 20 August 1883" (plate 93) is also unusually large in size (13 x 19 3/4 inches). It is rather carefully finished in color; the mountains are given all their contours; and there is relatively little indication of sky. But again the washes are very broad and loose: pink, greens, and ochers; the trees are drawn with long rapid lines, and the diary says: "Rose at 5. Perfectly clear. Health rather improving — but asthma still troubles me." In other words, the morning began as one of Lear's typical "better" days. "Came up [from drawing] by 10:30 & till noon penned out all I have pencilled here" (including, one presumes, the drawing under discussion). But then at luncheon "depressed & disgusted and besides I feel that I constantly grow weaker & weaker . . . bed by 8:15." In the end, the day closed sadly.

It would not add anything particular to this account if more examples of Lear's large later drawings and sketches were analyzed, nor are there a great many more at Harvard. Lear spent his last four years mainly working on and on at the Tennyson drawings. As Angus Davidson wrote, "So hopefully conceived thirty years before, the plan had now become a burden to him, and he continued his work on it more, perhaps, from obstinacy than from any conviction that his dream would be realized. 'I go on regularly at the A. T. illustrations' [Lear] wrote, 'vainly . . . seeking a method of doing them by which I can eventually multiply my 200 designs by photograph or autograph or sneezigraph . . .'" So by this time (1883) it is evident not only that the Tennyson project had become a fixation, but also that Lear had completed at least one full set of over two hundred drawings, which may be that recently rediscovered among the Tennyson papers now on deposit in the City Library at Lincoln, in England.

The first account of these drawings appeared in *Country Life* for October 8, 1964, in a very interesting article by M. R. Bruce illustrated with a few black and white reproductions. These show that each drawing has a border, and one is reminded that the passage quoted above from Lear's diary for August 14, 1879, says "all the outer frame lines are finished — & 2 of the narrow size penned out." Does this give us a date near the beginning of the Lincoln Tennyson series? There are no borders on the two smaller groups of drawings at Harvard which have just been briefly described. The Lincoln series of two hundred drawings is smaller in scale (about 3 3/4 x 5 3/4 inches) and is entirely in black and white wash. Two drawings are mounted on a sheet. Some drawings are touched with a dash of blue in places. None has any date inscribed. Many have the now familiar cypher of Lear's initials, and just two are inscribed by Lear "not to be autotyped." This note undoubtedly refers to what follows next.

Sometime about 1883, Lear commissioned a young artist named Frederick Underhill to help him translate the drawings he was making "by photograph, autograph, or sneezigraph" (actually, Underhill was a lithographer). The work on such drawings as Lear sent him proceeded very slowly. Moreover, Lear was quite evidently not satisfied. "*Nobody* can fully enter into my topographical notions and knowledge — and I am coming to the conclusion that unless I can get absolute facsimiles of my own work the whole thing must be given up," he wrote. But Lear could not give up: he had so little else to do. Therefore he dragged himself on.

Occasionally, as a release from this drudgery, between 1881 and 1885 he made other colored drawings of earlier large sketches on commission, or simply as a speculation. He mentioned in his diary for April 19, 1883, "Finished & packed in paper the last ten of the horrible 50 Corsicans [drawings of Corsica?] — much less 'finished' than they should be, — but human nature can no more"; and the next day, "Box with 97 Drawings going to Congreves for the Rail . . ." Was the view of Ajaccio (plate 94b;

4 3/4 x 7 1/4 inches) one of this "horrible" group? We cannot know; for like many later and smaller Lear drawings — even finished ones — it has no inscription of time, place, or date. One is forced to "date" it by the broad style of its washes, the few colors, the deep shadows of the reflections in the water, and the heavy paper Lear used more and more towards the end of his life. Fortunately, he gave all the information one could ask for on his drawing of "Sheikh Abou Fodde. 1867 Jany. 8" (plate 94a; 3 3/4 x 7 1/4 inches), signing it with his usual cypher, E.L., and the date of this copy, 1884. So here is another drawing, washed in with broad simple colors — blue, yellow, and gray, and with an atmospheric sky — by which we can judge the approximate date of the later unsigned ones. Lear's diary for January 8, 1867, says that "the long line of Abou Fodde is dreary grey," and he evidently did not forget to copy the notes on his original sketch; for it is all gray here. But the sails are luminous — even three-dimensional — and the reflections in the water are ably brought out by long vertical parallel lines in pen, and (for the sails) by blotches of Chinese white.

By 1885, at the latest, Lear started all over again to make a new series of two hundred drawings for Tennyson's poems, on a larger scale. These he eventually left to Lushington. Harvard now has this series, which W. B. O. Field bought in London about 1930, after the first Lushington sale. They are uniformly in black, gray, and white (the white partly blank paper, but partly also Chinese white for the most brilliant highlights, such as falling water in the sunshine). There are no dashes of color and on the whole the drawings are very somber, in keeping with Lear's general mood. He hoped they could be reproduced "somehow" but he was always in grave doubt, and he continued to consider young Underhill an uncertain asset. Normally, these drawings are on heavy paper like cardboard, one drawing to a page, roughly 6 x 10 inches, signed with Lear's cypher (but also the "AT" monogram that he invented) and numbered 1 to 200, rather roughly as was Lear's wont. Like a large Chinese collector's seal, the "AT" does not improve the composition and disturbs one's enjoyment, but Lear did not bother to think whether the "sneezigraph" could eliminate it. He was simply plodding on, wearily and patiently — living, as he said with a flash of his old wit, "in a mucilaginous monotony of submarine solitude," and worrying about his precarious financial status. (Money was always "a nabbomination to this child"; he had to send help "by sister Ellen to that poor foolish Texas brother [of his servant Giorgio] and . . . to a Nartist as is unphortschnit"; his agent's "gallery" in London — 129 Wardour Street — was not thriving, but he fervently hoped for "its success by little and little as the man said when he threw gunpowder in the fire.")

To judge from the diary, Lear called these Lushington-Harvard Tennyson drawings "chrysalises"; some previous sketches, "eggs." But in between he did some "insects." Are we to infer that the earlier Harvard drawings are "eggs," and the Lincoln drawings "insects"? In any event, he says that he finished the last of the "eggs" on January 19, 1885, and on May 1 he seems to have become discouraged with "insects"; for he writes: "Worked a good deal — first at the A. T. insect 'the English home'; 2nd at 'the Moonlight on still waters' [the titles are both extracts from Tennyson poems] but neither pleased me & finally at 6 p.m. I am half inclined to try simple black chalk & white — for if the whole lot are to be only done in monotint — the labour of color is useless." Thereafter, although he drew a few more "insects" he took up the "black & white [chrysalis] A. T.s" in earnest, "washing and sloshing" them (over black charcoal or pencil outlines) till on November 24, 1885, he "wound up the [*this* series of] A. T.s generally."

A view of Palaeocastritza, Corfu (plate 97; 6 1/4 x 10 1/4 inches) is a good example of what I take to be the "chrysalis" type. Pencil was doubtless used for the first outlines, which may have been tracings of previous drawings, but charcoal seems certainly indicated by some intense blacks. Over the preliminary drawing a final wash has been laid, and in some drawings Chinese white is used for the highlights. Was the drawing of Palaeocastritza made by Lear in 1863 (plate 62; 13 1/2 x 22 3/4 inches) the original large-scale drawing? Is the smaller-scale view from almost exactly the same position, without the figures and in color (plate 96; 5 1/4 x 10 1/4 inches), the "egg" for this "new" Tennyson subject? The drawing shown in plate 96 is almost exactly the same size as that shown in plate 97 and it could have been used to furnish a tracing on which Lear changed the details, as was his custom. Topographical accuracy was no longer essential in the illustrations for Tennyson, since Lear was long past caring for minor matters as he laboriously struggled through the summer and autumn of 1885.

"Barrackpur, India" (plate 98; 6 1/4 x 10 1/4 inches) is much more original in style. It has a most unusual feature of ocher wash added over the gray of the spreading boughs on the great trees. The huge trees of "Barrackpoor" (plate 84; 10 1/2 x 17 inches), dated 1873, seem to be the earlier model for this drawing. If one reads the captions from Tennyson's poems which Lear's drawings are supposed to illustrate, one sees that he interpreted the poet rather freely. He even occasionally misquotes his lines!

Yet he is still capable of a striking drawing, as "Capo S. Angelo, Amalfi" (plate 99; 6 1/4 x 10 1/4 inches) demonstrates. It is the angry, dark sea that makes this drawing impressive — a rather stormier sea than we have ever observed before. Tired as he was, Lear seemed still to be able to improvise, although there is no assurance that he had not drawn some such sea in a sketch of this subject earlier. He had done so in the case of "Finale" (plate 64), which is much more successful than the later drawing reproduced as plate 101 (6 1/4 x 10 1/4 inches).

"Lake Lugano, Switzerland" (plate 100; 6 1/4 x 10 1/4 inches) is in an even stormier, more abstract vein, though without waves. It would have almost the effect of a Turner if only the washes were more ably handled. It is nearly as far from the detailed, peaceful views of Lear's youth as the later Turners are from the early ones. But Lear was not attuned to storms, and peace returns in "Paestum" (plate 103; 6 1/4 x 10 1/4 inches) and in "Mount Athos" (plate 102; 6 1/2 x 10 inches), both of which were surely copied from earlier sketches. In the artist's diary entry for January 26, 1885, he says (apropos of "Paestum") that he was "looking out for temple sketches to go on with now that all the Palms are done." For Lear did not make these Tennyson drawings in sequence of captions ("Paestum" is number 68) but by subjects, such as "mountains," and "scenes along the Nile, etc." On February 15, he was looking for sketches of "Naples, Constantinople & Campagna — 'all things fair'," and one may be sure his cabinets and portfolios at San Remo were as full of them as those same cabinets are now at Harvard.

Whether Lear made many drawings of *English* landscapes in his earlier years is not clear from Harvard's holdings. All the writer can say is that the Lushington Tennyson monochrome series contains a fair number of English subjects, of which "Beachy Head" (plate 104; 6 1/2 x 10 inches), with its stormy sky and its running sea, is a fair example. But it is with the monochrome wash rendering of the "Coast of Travancore, India" (plate 105; 6 1/2 x 10 inches) that this series should end, so far as subject matter is concerned. It is dark, lonely, and as abandoned in its mood as Lear so often felt personally at the end of his life. There is no drawing in the "chrysalis" (monochrome) series that is dated other — or later — than 1885, although a few like the "Capo S. Angelo, Amalfi" drawing (plate 99) are undated. It is almost certain from reading Lear's diary page by page for the entire year that they were all executed in about six months, from May to the end of November, 1885.

Despite the completion of this full series of two hundred "chrysalis" drawings, a new group in still larger size was begun as late as April 1887. And on July 28, after he had passed "a dreadful night XXX" (the X's, as always, mean attacks of "the Demon"), Lear once again worked till "7 pm or so, at no. 118 Mt. Athos." "I don't even yet know whether it will be possible even to make it a decent drawing," he sadly concluded. Another entry about "the A. Ts." was on August 8: "Shall look over the 200 (monochrome) A. T.s again I think . . ." And, finally, on August 12th he wrote a letter of thanks for a

volume of them that he had loaned. Then silence. We have no diary evidence that he ever worked on "the A. T.s" again, or on any other drawing, in the five months of life which still remained to him. These late Tennyson drawings (1887) have disappeared; will they reappear as did the drawings at Lincoln? Or, should I say, *have* they reappeared at Messrs. Agnew in London, bought at Sir Osbert Sitwell's sale, March 3, 1965?

In this sale there were fifty-two landscape drawings of several sizes, almost all quite large. The majority are approximately 10 x 20 inches — a few of them even 12 x 20, but there are some 9 x 14, and still fewer 6 x 10 and 4 x 7. The subjects are almost surely for Tennyson, although they are not marked with the "A.T." device. The subjects covered are from Corsica, Egypt, Switzerland, Italy, Greece, India, England, Albania, Turkey, and Syria — all countries, as we have seen, that attracted Lear for this purpose. The drawings are contained in an album. The media used are chiefly pen, ink, pencil, and sepia wash, but sometimes watercolor has been added. A small group is in strong red ink. All are rather freely and loosely drawn, as would have been necessary for Lear thus late in his life. Is this, in fact, the last group begun in 1887? Until some documentary evidence turns up there is no way of telling. In Lear's last months, as I said in the first section of this book, he wrote very little, and in his diary hardly at all.

Just after Lear's death on January 29, 1888, a memorial volume in honor of their old friend was initiated by Tennyson and his wife. It contained three poems by the Poet Laureate, with twenty-two reduced facsimiles of Lear's monochrome ("chrysalis"?) drawings and a four-page essay by Lushington. Boussod, Valadon Co. of Paris & London was the European publisher; Scribner & Welford, in New York, the American one. Supposedly only one hundred copies were issued by Tennyson, of which the Field Collection at Harvard has one. However, a special copy belonging to the writer is *not* numbered, and carries the words "extra copy for Presentation." It is inscribed to "Franklin Lushington from Tennyson and Emily Tennyson," in the poet's handwriting. In a sense this is the dedication copy, since Lear was dead and Lushington was his residuary legatee. No other use of the Tennyson drawings has yet been made, as far as the writer is aware. They would make, if the poorer ones were eliminated, a very interesting and dramatic publication to demonstrate the late but real advance Lear made in his use of abstract forms and atmospheric effects during his last, dark years at San Remo.

The Relation of Lear's Drawing to His Painting

V

THE INFLUENCE OF LEAR'S DRAWING on his painting is reasonably direct. His paintings — with few exceptions — were ultimately derived from his quick, "on the spot" pencil or pen sketches. But there were usually some intermediate steps. As we have already noted, there was almost invariably a "penned out" drawing made from the first sketch or sketches. Then quite often a "finished" drawing was made from the "penned out" one, for sale, or on commission. Lear endlessly repeated the subjects that pleased him most. He was especially prone to redraw — and repaint — certain views in places where he had lived for a long time during his more active years. Lady Strachey cites 292 "paintings" from a list Lear drew up at San Remo in 1877 for circulation as an advertisement among his friends and prospective patrons. (He was proud of the range of his painting in both size and subject, and prouder still of certain names that could be noticed among the purchasers.)

In this list of 1877 we find no less than eleven paintings showing the Citadel of Corfu as seen from a vantage point near the village of Ascension; the writer owns one of these, done about 1858 (plate 107; 14 3/4 x 9 1/2 inches). In addition, Lear's list mentions three "paintings" from "below Ascension." This large number may open the actual medium of the pictures to doubt. Is it possible that all these views are really oils? Or may they (as the writer suspects) include highly finished colored drawings? Lear's oils were not popular, and he had an incentive to make his list as long and as impressive as possible. In his later years he became mixed up in his memories, mislabeling and misdating on occasion, as can sometimes be proved. His statements cannot always be taken literally.

Altogether, Harvard has over a dozen different sizes of Corfu drawings that resemble the painting owned by the writer. The closest one, reproduced as plate 41 (12 x 20 3/4 inches), carries neither time nor date. A comparison of the painting and this sketch, barely "penned out," with no color, shows that it might be the earliest source for the painting, but there is no telling how many other drawings may have been made in between.

The finished drawing of "Petra" (1858) belonging to the writer (plate 57) is closer still to a painting (plate 109; 36 x 60 inches) owned in 1939 by Mrs. R. C. Gillies, a collateral relative of Lear's in New Zealand and now by Mr. Craig Gillies of Lear House, Oamaru, New Zealand. Here we may have the final step from drawing to painting, but, of course, we cannot be sure.

Lear never tells us how long he worked and how many, and which, steps he took in his derivation. He wanted his paintings all to seem "inspired," but one can see that they rarely were. A small painting of Mount Parnassus (plate 48; 9 1/4 x 14 3/4 inches), owned by the writer, has every flowery spike of asphodel and every sheep in the foreground perfectly delineated. Even the snowy mountain is shown in the greatest detail. All that

is missing is life, air, and atmosphere! The scene seems caught with telescopic and photographic exactitude, but one wonders whether it is not a highly imaginative elaboration of an elaboration, based on Lear's diary notes and on one of the "penned out" sketches in his reference collection, far back in the sequence of drawing studies. The writer has yet to see an oil painting for which he has reason to doubt that there is, or was, a reasonably comparable drawing. Such a painting or such paintings may exist, to be sure, but the number of them is apt to be small. One piece of supporting evidence is the fact that many more drawings turn up nowadays than paintings, even though a ready market for the paintings, saving only the largest ones, has come into being. If there were a great mass of Lear paintings still in private hands, we should know it by now. This argument only heightens the probability that Lear's list of 1877 includes finished drawings as well as oil paintings. "Janina" (plate 56; 7 1/8 x 14 7/8 inches), and even more likely, "Thermopylae" (plate 47) may be examples of these.

One of the exceptions to a general sense of lifelessness in Lear's paintings is an unfinished oil sketch of olive trees (plate 106; 18 x 23 inches), which appeared on the London market early in 1964, with two other similar studies of palm trees. This oil, on a cream-colored prepared surface over a cardboard base, is full of vitality and seems to have been painted almost "free hand," with a minimum of preliminary pen lines. Lear has dated it on the back "1858," which suggests that it may have been done in Corfu, as do the very tall as well as ancient olive trees themselves. Another fine free oil sketch of Corfu was shown in the Arts Council of Great Britain 1958 exhibition (number 5 in the catalogue), and there are undoubtedly some others here and there. These oils may have been made directly on the spot, or without any preliminary sketches on paper. The drawing underneath the painting is in pen lines — very quick and incisive. The writer has an oil view of Girgenti in Sicily of the same nature, labeled "Acragas" and dated "May 1847."

In respect to the general run of Lear's finished oils (*not* these) one should recall what Lear said to his great friend Chichester Fortescue, as reported by Davidson and others: "Yes, I certainly *do* hate the act of painting, and although day after day I go steadily on it is like grinding my nose off." He took too much — or too little — advice from his friend William Holman Hunt: too much when he endeavored to put the Pre-Raphaelite finish and detail into his painting, and too little when he refused to change his habit of painting from sketches and drawings made long in the past. Lear confessed to Hunt, as he did to Fortescue, that he frequently broke down "with despair" when he painted. "To speak candidly," Hunt replied, "I could not, and would not [even] attempt to paint pictures in a studio from such mere skeleton outlines." *

When Lear made his first "on the spot" drawings his psychological attitude was quite different. Then he usually worked with enthusiasm and vigor: the nearer the time of the first sketch, the stronger and surer the result. Yet even in his last days, as we have seen with some of the Tennyson illustrations, he occasionally rendered an old drawing in a new and imaginative way, despite the fact that he was plodding along without much plan or much hope. Undoubtedly he truly longed to honor his friend, but he also desperately needed to keep busy in order to forget himself.

* W. H. Hunt, *Pre-Raphaelitism and the Pre-Raphaelite Brotherhood* (London, 1905), I, 328.

*An Estimate of Lear as a
Landscape Draughtsman*

VI

It is curious that no extensive appraisal of the merits and defects of Lear's landscape drawings and sketches seems to have been attempted. In Lady Strachey's first volume of Lear's *Letters*, an appreciation of him as a *painter* by her brother, Henry Strachey, occupies a little under five pages, from which the writer has already quoted. Angus Davidson, of course, has also made some excellent general observations in a chapter of his biography, and in *Teapots and Quails*. Hubert Congreve wrote a bit about Lear as an artist in Lady Strachey's *Later Letters*; and there have been other individual comments, such as Lushington's, Robert Wark's, and Brian Reade's. But a general consideration of the landscape drawings picturing the many fascinating countries in which Lear spent by far the greatest part of his life has somehow been overlooked. It will be the last task of this book to offer the writer's personal estimate of their significance. This will doubtless not satisfy every reader by any means; in the end, each individual must make up his own mind on the subject. But what follows is the result of considerable thought based on the study of a very large number of drawings in the United States, and of a few collections in England.

From a positive point of view it can surely be claimed that Lear was one of the ablest *topographical* draughtsmen of his day. Sometimes he was more than that, as has been demonstrated in the consideration of individual drawings; for he was more "creative" and more "classic" than has generally been admitted. Capable of rapid, powerful preliminary sketches, he was also able to tell a great deal about a scene in a very few lines. As his nonsense drawings amply prove, Lear was excellent at "shorthand." When he felt more methodically inclined, he was able to render every detail with almost microscopic clarity. Not only do many of his "penned out" landscape drawings show this ability, but so do his earlier natural history drawings. Perhaps it is a pity that he "penned out" so much and then made copies from copies, but to these copies he sometimes added a creative clarity of vision—when he felt reasonably well, or when his memories, evoked by the sketch and his written notes, came back vividly. We have seen that a vivid memory could last for a long time in the case of the scene at "Roorkee, March 20, 1874" (plate 79), which was not "penned out and colored" till September 1876. Perhaps the representation is no longer quite accurate in fact, but it does have an authority of presentation and feeling.

Lear was able to show geological strata and the mass content within the outer form of mountains better than almost any other artist of the century. As Henry Strachey observed in his sister's *Letters of Edward Lear*, "A traveller could almost plan his route over a pass from one of this artist's faithful realizations of mountains" (see "Cattaro," plate 69, and "Forest of Bavella, Corsica," plate 72). Layer upon layer of an eroded ancient rocky land shows in the drawing of "Petra" (plate 57), and—Henry Strachey again—"If he painted the Roman Campagna every sinew in the plain was lovingly recorded

. . . every arch of the aqueducts" ("Ponte Sant' Antonio," plate 21). In "Kôm Ombo" (plate 52), he portrays every detail of the stones of fallen masonry in the foreground.

The inner grace and nature of trees comes out continually, all the way from "Tivoli, 1838" (plate 11) to the avenue of palms in "Calicut" (plate 83), thirty-six years later. If Lear "painted an olive tree near at hand against the sky," he did not always "count the leaves," as Henry Strachey implies; he was able to render the massed foliage quite freely. He does so particularly well in the oil sketch of "Olive Trees, 1858" (plate 106). The tropical foliage of "Hanwele, Ceylon, 1874" (plate 85) is actually quite impressionistic in certain passages, while the pine trees of "Abetone, 1883" (plate 93) rear their heads in a starkly simplified and dramatic formation. When Lear's eyesight really began to lose its sharpness he was forced to generalize, but sometimes his "penned out" drawings then acquired a new, long-lacking abstraction or simplicity of expression, as witness "Assisi, 1883" (plate 90). Occasionally, as in his early view of "Passerano, 1843" (plate 18), he created a nearly pure watercolor of lyric beauty, as free and as uncomplicated, if not as powerful, as one could find in the work of his better-known contemporaries. But to work in color and pure tonal values combined never became a habit of his, more's the pity!

At its best, Lear's normal coloring was sparing, sober, and subtle. Bright, freely washed colors were clearly neither to his taste nor suited to his talent. Yet he always strove to give his drawings mood, and a feeling for the time of the day. Generally his washes were light in hue and soft in tone, with a preference for violet, gray, and blue. Ocher is also frequent, and the more delicate shades of green. But sometimes, both early and late, he confined his color to the minimum, as witness "Palermo, 1842" (plate 17) and "Assisi, 1883" (plate 90). In contrast, sometimes — usually later — his colors are dark and menacing, as in "Mount Athos, 1856" (plate 54); or even striking, as in "Roorkee, 1874" (plate 79).

The wide view of "Zante, 1848" (frontispiece) is the most brilliantly and elaborately colored drawing of all that are reproduced in this book, but it is the writer's opinion that this highly finished composition should be considered an intermediate step toward a painting. Every olive leaf is here counted indeed, and every hair on the goats' backs. In sum, it is a dramatic "tour de force," just saved by the fact that it still is a colored drawing with some unfinished passages and a more than usually atmospheric sky.

Very highly in Lear's favor should be considered the fact that he is one of the few, as well as one of the best, artists who show the Mediterranean lands in that enchanting state of wilderness superimposed on ruins of ancient civilization which they had reached when Lear visited them. The charm and the sadness in no way escaped him; his lonely spirit felt an intimate kinship with what he saw, and he was able to express it. Who else has drawn such scenes so well? Does he not, for example, give us the Greece of our dreams — the Greece that *was* once, but is now so quickly changing? No one else — not Harding, not Pars, not Müller — has portrayed it so sympathetically. No wonder, then, that those who know the wonderful Greek sketches by Lear in the Gennadius Library at Athens pore over them and seek the few of his Greek subjects perhaps more eagerly than any others which come on the market today!

The immense productivity of Lear's long years as a draughtsman has often been commented upon, but it cannot be too often admired or, contrariwise, dismissed "as more and more about less and less." Even the Tennyson drawings of his last years have a value of their own and a more than occasional originality that is unexpected. Even when the artist was most careless, as he often was in these last years, drawing and redrawing from scenes of long before, one never feels that he is unfeeling or insincere. If a view of Mount Sinai made for Tennyson's *Poems* in 1885 is but an ill-drawn shadow of the strong sketch of 1849 (plate 40) or of the highly finished drawing of 1869 (plate 39; 7 x 15 inches), which the writer owns, it is still as carefully rendered as Lear's health, strength, and eyesight would permit. Lear always took infinite pains, from the first sketches we have seen until the last months of his life when he "started A. T.s all over again." Such patience is rarely characteristic of artists today; such sincerity not always present in the paintings and drawings of the masters in the current abstract movement.

Still we must now consider Lear's obvious and less obvious faults. The most noticeable one is probably his frequent lack of spontaneity. So often unwell, and working so continuously away from the scene of his sketches, he made a multitude of *dry* landscape drawings. Very few of his drawings have atmospheric qualities. Lear put a bold face on the name "topographical draughtsman" — he even claimed it proudly — but he was surely aware that this approach was far from the spirit of his most admired British master, Turner.

Stiffness and lifelessness characterized nearly all his large paintings and many of his smaller ones, as well as certain highly finished drawings. He had a terrible tendency to insert more and more unnecessary detail — detail that was not even true to fact, though Lear would never have realized it or thought of it from such a point of view. His notes, his memories, seemed vivid and accurate to him. He would doubtless have denied that his drawings and paintings could contain topographical errors; he was quite sure they contained every essential truth. For example, however, two small paintings of Mount Athos (one owned by the writer and the other now owned by Michael Coe) are obviously derived from the same sketch or finished drawing, but Lear has changed all sorts of details, and even certain contours on the mountain itself. Which version is accurate, if either is? One would probably have to go back to the very first sketch to be reasonably sure.

It has already been clearly stated that Lear was not a watercolorist, except on very rare occasions, when he produced such sketches as "Passerano, 20 October 1843" (plate 18). Still, some of the Tennyson monochromes are closely related to watercolors, since they are constructed of washes with a brush and have very few lines. Almost all the rest of Lear's drawings now at Harvard — and others elsewhere, the writer suspects — are drawn in line and colored or washed in with tonal passages afterwards, in the eighteenth-century manner.

Lear was essentially a traditionalist, as cannot too often be emphasized. Having found a personal style, he clung to it, regardless of new fashions and new optical discoveries. The Impressionist movement passed him completely by. What Impressionism there is in his late drawings came from his failing eyesight more than from any attempt to fall into tune with the times. A tragic sense of loneliness and darkness increasingly dominated his thoughts and was reflected in the Tennyson drawings. "Travancore," number 181 of the monochrome Tennysons (plate 105) is much less representative of the southeast coast of India (near Madras — near Lear's nonsense favorite "Coast of Coromandel, where the early pumpkins blow") than of some northern coastline in winter during a storm. The two little sailing craft in

"Travancore" are more like Arab river boats than sea-going Indian vessels. Nevertheless, here is a dramatic scene with a sense of doom about it. One cannot see the coast for the dark mist; one doubts that the ships will ever make shore. The writer is reminded of Victor Hugo's haunted, stormy, monochrome watercolors in the museum which was once his house on the Place des Vosges in Paris.

In spite of the relative success of this "Travancore" wash drawing, Lear was rarely interested in, or able to render turbulent seas or stormy clouds. Nearly all his drawings show serene skies, and quiet water full of reflections. His drawings are almost still-lifes, caught at a moment when nothing moved. There is rarely action; the figures are usually contemplative or reflective — like Lear in his own many quiet moods. With the exception of his notes to himself, there is almost no humor — and this from one of the most truly humorous authors who ever lived! The drawings are deadly serious, and the people have far less life than the birds in the wonderful ornithological drawings of his youth.

We have observed that Lear sometimes made studies of people, particularly in the Levant, where the costumes fascinated him (Berat, plate 36), but he never really mastered life drawings so that he was wholly at ease with them. He was more successful with ships, especially when they were seen from afar. He loved dawn and dusk — the moments when nature was at rest, when the wind did not blow, when the trees and rocks stood out in the greatest clarity of definition.

Sunrise and sunset effects greatly interested Lear, but he was not often successful with them. Some of his worst failures are attempts to depict the red, "hot" sunsets of the tropics; he washed on great smears of carmine, pink, purple, and orange in desperate abandon, hoping to catch the uncatchable, the exact second of the most dramatic effect. There are some that are truly dreadful. So are his rainbows, and a view (from near Catania) of Aetna in violent eruption. This has no verisimilitude whatsoever; for imagination (in landscape) was not Lear's strong point. Again this seems strange, when one recalls the exquisite humorous imagination of his nonsense poems. Occasionally, too, Lear becomes over sentimental, as in a late view, now at Harvard, of what seems to be northern Greece (Mount Olympus?), where a dying swan is seen in the center of the placid river in the foreground. Lear's melancholy often broke into his drawings. Only in his "nonsenses" is his childlike yearning for gaiety and fun predominant, and never even there for very long.

The failure of Lear to study the work of his contemporaries and most of the masters of the past, despite his own admonition — to study Turner after "the works of the Almighty," as reported by Henry Strachey — should be counted against Lear in this summary. Turner lived till 1851, and Lear could, and should, have profited from the great Turner atmospheric watercolors and paintings of 1843–1851. Once again, one must lay this failure both to Lear's insecurity and to his conservative nature. He was ever fearful of failure, and tended to draw only what he was *sure* he could master quickly. Is this why he did not meet Turner when they both were in London, or because Turner himself became a recluse? And why did Lear learn nothing from John Constable's masterpieces, which must have been talked of and shown at the moment of that great artist's death in 1837? (This was the year when Lear, having determined to become a landscape painter, set off for Rome.) If it was because Constable drew only English subjects, still Lear could have profited in his own English period (1834–1837) from Constable's superb views of Hampstead Heath and East Anglia, which were so often drawn from the same kind of vantage point as Lear chose for himself. And John Robert Cozens' glorious watercolors from Italy, near Rome, should have inspired Lear to do more than simply to go there. Indeed, had Lear been willing (and not perhaps just insecure or jealous), he could have profited in many other ways if he had studied the atmosphere, the composition, and the color of the English watercolorists before and of his own time.

There is little indication of seasons in Lear's views, mainly because the outward manifestations of seasonal change in the Mediterranean lands are not obvious. But in this fact lies another reason that one feels too great a sense of uniformity in his drawings. To be sure, his variations of scenes are considerable in subject, manner of drawing, coloring, and scale, but little in weather, time of day, type of foreground, and mood. Architecture, like people, is either minimized or dramatized, but rarely studied for itself. Portraiture is almost nonexistent. Lear's towns nearly all resemble one another in many details and nearly all are shown with an effort to find the "picturesque" in the fashion of his youth. And so he went on looking for the "picturesque" and the "poetic" in nature to the very end of his days, but finding all too many types rather than individual features.

Sir Kenneth Clark, in his essay *On the Painting of English Landscape*, a British Academy Lecture in 1935, calls attention to the special quality of English landscape which results from the uniting of the picturesque with topography, but adds that its artists were "seldom content to draw their inspiration direct" from their native countryside. He was alluding to Cozens, to Girtin, and to Turner in his earlier years. But he could just as well have meant Lear. "Picturesque topography" served Lear all his life. The English climate was physically hard on him, and it also became unsympathetic. Passionately as he needed home and security, he needed to wander still more, in order to overcome claustrophobia, boredom, and the demands of a conservative society. So he explored continuously here and there, always seeking something different and never *quite* finding it. He did try to look at new views with a new eye, but he rarely succeeded. He varied his scenes all he could, but they came down in the end to all too much that was the same.

At his best incisive, classic, austere, or nostalgic and perceptive; at his worst sentimental and repetitive, Lear continued steadily on his chosen path, never looking aside to other artists or to newer trends. The end result is still quite impressive: a great corpus of drawings from parts of northern Europe and nearly every Mediter-ranean land, from India and from Ceylon, with some early views in the British Isles. Although his own life was relieved by humor and occasionally by wit, he should have allowed his playful and inventive side more rein in his landscape drawing. Here he was overly plodding and serious. But there is no other artist of his time to show us so lovingly and so painstakingly within the framework of the Victorian spirit these then unspoilt lands.

The Growth in Appreciation of
Lear's Landscape Drawings
VII

IN BRYAN's *Dictionary of Painters and Engravers* (London, 1910; III, 190–191) occurs the following *misinformation* about the artist who is the subject of this book — a widely gifted genius, sure to be recognized in the end as one of the most interesting figures of the English nineteenth century:

"LEAR, Edward, draughtsman and landscape painter, was born in 1813(?) on the Earl of Derby's estate near Knowsley, in Lancashire, his father being an employee of the Earl. He was the youngest of twenty-one children, and by the help of friends was enabled to become an accurate zoological draughtsman . . . Lear never became popular, however, as a landscape painter, and in his later years he can scarcely be said to have risen above the rank of a topographical artist . . ."

These highly inaccurate and derogatory lines were printed just over twenty years after the artist-writer's death, while at least a *dozen* people of prominence were still alive who knew him well, including Evelyn Baring, Earl Cromer, one of the most respected statesmen in England. Lear had given painting lessons to Queen Victoria. His oils and drawings were scattered all over the British Isles. He exhibited in the Royal Academy from 1850 to 1873. Given these facts, is it not strange that a reference book considered standard could make so many mistakes in so few lines? The only correct statement is that his *paintings* were not generally popular in his own day!

Nevertheless, by 1910 a revival of interest in Lear had already begun. Its first important manifestation was Lady Strachey's *Letters of Edward Lear* (London, 1907), which went quickly through four editions by 1910. A second volume of letters under her editorship — *Later Letters of Edward Lear* — came out in 1911. Both of these have been quoted from, and both were illustrated with reproductions of scores of the artist's drawings and paintings. Lady Strachey also included a number of appendices presenting detailed information about almost five hundred of Lear's pictures as well as about nearly all his illustrated travel journals and works on ornithology. Lear's friends, in a word, were still enthusiastic, even though the majority of contemporary critics were unimpressed.

By 1929, however, nearly all Lear's personal friends had died. Yet suddenly, in February and March of that year, there came several remarkable auction sales at Hodgson's and Sotheby's in London which included a large number of his drawings, manuscripts, books, prints, and the thirty volumes of a personal diary left in his Villa at San Remo which he had bequeathed to Sir Franklin Lushington. These sales took place by the order or Sir Franklin's daughters. Three months later the writer purchased in a London bookshop a scrapbook with over fifty landscape drawings, dozens of nonsense sketches, and seven manuscript poems for the absurdly low figure of sixty pounds! No demand from the British

collecting world had yet developed. The bookseller's shelves, in fact, were glutted — and this in a year of high prosperity throughout the English-speaking world, when some English nineteenth century "first editions" reached an all-time high in market value.

The Howard Gallery in London held an exhibition from October 21 to November 9, 1929, in which fifty-seven Lear drawings, purchased by Messrs. Craddock and Barnard, were offered at prices ranging from three to ten guineas, but this was not a success. Too many more watercolors were available at the same gallery and others, lying loose in portfolios. An article in the *Morning Post*, October 31, 1929, noted that the drawings would "be a surprise to most who see them [because] they appear to claim for the artist a more assured place among our water-colourists than is generally recognized." Such recognition took its time in arriving. In the course of the next several years, a large number of Lear's drawings were sold at even lower prices — as low as five shillings each — to intelligent collectors like Mr. Joannes Gennadius and Mr. Henry C. Smith of E. P. Dutton and Company, New York, on behalf of his friend, Mr. William B. Osgood Field.

On November 27, 1929, Sotheby's sold a portion of the Earl of Northbrook's Lear collection, which was to prove even larger than Lushington's. This sale compounded the problem of disposal by the dealers. But by this time Mr. Field importantly, and the writer less actively, were buying for their own collections in New York. They became friends, and this development led, in time, to the present Lear collection in the Department of Graphic Arts of the Harvard College Library, although it was early in 1942 before the material was brought together through simultaneous gifts at the opening of the Houghton Library. Mr. Field continued to purchase Lear drawings and books during the 1930's; his greatest acquisition, the main lot of Northbrook landscape drawings in two large walnut cabinets, took place after 1932.

The real turning point in a general appreciation of Edward Lear *as an artist*, however, came in London in 1938. It was then that John Murray published Angus Davidson's biography, deservedly praised and cited in nearly all the preceding chapters. In the same year R. L. Mégroz published an article in the *Cornhill Magazine*; The Fine Arts Society (on Bond Street, London) organized a successful exhibition of Lear's landscape watercolors, and Duckworth published Granville Proby's *Lear in Sicily*. This last-named book, to be sure, had a series of twenty nonsense drawings as its main theme, but the artistic side of Lear, and his traveling companion of 1847, John Joshua Proby, figure largely, and the frontispiece is a reproduction in color of a Lear landscape. Meanwhile, in 1933, Bertha Coolidge Slade's magnificent 455-page catalogue of the Field Collection, *Edward Lear on My Shelves*, had been printed in Germany and published privately by Mr. Field in New York. Since this book was mainly given (not sold) to Mr. Field's personal friends, it was not generally known for some time in England, where the main knowledge of Lear lingered and the chief incentive to study him was bound to awaken, as it did so notably in 1938.

Then came Brian Reade's ornithological article in *Signature* (1947), followed by his equally specialized, excellent, illustrated monograph, *Edward Lear's Parrots* (London: Duckworth, 1949) and a slowly mounting series of other critical notices. Angus Davidson and the writer edited some nonsense material which had been gradually uncovered at Harvard, *Teapots and Quails* (London: John Murray, 1953), calling attention to Lear's varied artistic talents. Five years later Philip James and Brian Reade wrote admirable essays for the catalogue of the Lear exhibition sponsored by the Arts Council of Great Britain (London, 1958).

In 1962 Robert R. Wark wrote an excellent six-page introduction to the Huntington Library's exhibition catalogue, *Drawings by Edward Lear*. In 1964, a loan exhibition of Lear's watercolors was sent from England to Corfu in the Greek Ionian Islands, where Lear spent so much time, and in this same year the Graves Art Gallery, in Sheffield, England, exhibited fifty-four landscape drawings of Lear's, mainly from the Hollis family and the collection of Lieutenant Colonel C. J. B. Church. On October 8, 1964, an article appeared in *Country Life* about the drawings for Tennyson's poems, newly rediscovered in the City Library of Lincoln. These are not all the notices Lear, the artist, has more recently received, but they are some of the principal ones and indicate the trend of thoughtful opinion which is now beginning to give him his due.

But Edward Lear, the greatest English nonsense writer of the nineteenth century, has had difficulty in emerging as a serious artist. That he has come as far as he has results more from the eagerness of collectors than from the aid of scholars and critics, for up to this moment no knowledgeable critic has made a comprehensive study of his landscape drawings. As for Lear's painting, his avowed profession, really nothing at all has appeared! From the artistic viewpoint his nonsense drawings have never been critically examined nor their influence weighed. His diaries from 1858 to his death thirty years later are still unedited, although they are available at Harvard. Other, earlier, diaries may exist, and more journals (besides the published Indian Journal) remain to be rediscovered. And there is still no scholarly analysis of Lear's verse, although David McCord, the American poet, who is fitted by familiarity and understanding to bring this facet of his genius into perspective, still hopes to find time to make such a study.

But today museum directors and curators are rediscovering Lear drawings that have lain neglected on their shelves. A multitude of new collectors have appeared, among whom museum men are not absent. Greeks are prominent in this wave of interest, despite prices which are up to a thousandfold what Mr. Gennadius paid thirty years ago. Sales seem now only limited by the supply on the market. In the next pages some general idea of the spreading interest Lear's landscape drawings have aroused will be attempted.

Present Status of
Lear Collections

VIII

It is quite clear that Edward Lear's landscape drawings are his largest serious artistic contribution to posterity. (The nonsense drawings are not weighed in this statement because they were not intended to be serious, although they are very important.) It was estimated by Hubert Congreve, an artist, friend, and pupil of Lear, in his preface to Lady Strachey's *Later Letters of Edward Lear*, that at his death Lear left "over 10,000 large cardboard sheets of sketches." This estimate, I think, is too high; for there seem to be no collections anywhere recorded of more than several hundred drawings, except the group at Harvard, which is more than three thousand four hundred; but a proportion of these are relatively small drawings, with sometimes as many as eighteen on a single cardboard sheet. The group at Harvard contains few highly finished subjects, except the two hundred relatively well-developed monochrome drawings for Tennyson's *Poems.* I, however, have a score of finished drawings — of the type Lear sold to clients — which would not seem to have been included in Congreve's estimate, nor in his words "large cardboard sheets of sketches." Emphatically "10,000 sheets" looks too high; I doubt if there are ten thousand separate Lear drawings of the various types and sizes altogether.

One reason for this opinion is that another statement in this same book can almost certainly be proved to be exaggerated. Lady Strachey in her editor's note says of Lear's collateral descendants, the Gillies family in New

Zealand, that "they possess vast stores of Lear's drawings." This overstates the fact. By dint of hard work, and the very kind assistance of Lady Gillies, widow of Sir Harold Gillies, now living in London, and Craig Gillies of Lear House, Oamaru, New Zealand, I can now quote the latter's letter to me, October 27, 1966, as follows: "It is a sad story — Emily Gillies, my grand-mother was to have been Edward Lear's beneficiary, but this did not eventuate for several reasons. The Lushingtons, however, sent her, *amongst other things*, about three hundred watercolour drawings and sketches. Certain of Emily's children at various times were given [several] watercolours each from this collection; my father (Robert) had two, Arthur nil, Harry nil, Aunt Emily (married Dr. Michel of Cambridge University, England) about six. Her son Bobby *lives* in England, but I have an idea her Lears went to Aunt Lilly in Capetown, S.A. etc. . . . But some of [the] Lears seem to be unaccounted for, as Dr. E. L. Gillies has only about four or five [although] John A. Gillies has some very good ones from his father Harold . . . On my grand-mother's death approximately three hundred watercolours came to my father and then to me. Oh, sadness! [How like Edward Lear himself this expression is!] These three hundred were destroyed in a fire in 1937, while in storage. The few I now have [were luckily not there]. My Aunt Lill was the Lear enthusiast of her generation [Mrs. E. L. Bowen in S.A.] . . . but . . . on her death there was little Lear material

in evidence, and I have never been able to get any satisfactory explanation of its fate . . . I lost Lear manuscripts and personal items as well as watercolours in the fire disaster, but have increasingly collected Lear items as and when possible and am keen to have more."

Clearly Craig Gillies in New Zealand has some fine Lear drawings and sketches again as well as the large oil painting of Petra (plate 109), but not a collection to overtop those in England, Greece, and America, a summary account of which will shortly follow. Nor do any other Lear collateral relatives seem to have more than the "four or five" drawings which Craig Gillies' letter to me states. To be sure, possibly Dr. Edward Lear Gillies, who lives at Levin, New Zealand, may have a fair "number of drawings bequeathed to him by [his aunt] Mrs. E. L. Bowen," as reported to me by John A. Gillies, in a letter of October 14, 1965, which would account for her holdings about which Craig Gillies was not quite sure, and Lady Gillies in London possesses a few watercolors, and a fine oil sketch of Corfu (on paper varnished) loaned to the 1958 British Council, London, exhibition, but these collections are still in the range of a few drawings, not many. And although the Gillies relatives of Lear live now in as remote spots as Baghdad, as well as in England and New Zealand, we can probably dismiss the idea that there is a huge treasure trove of Lear drawings in their hands.

Harvard's Lear holdings, therefore, are almost surely

the most numerous and important of any in one place. They are also the principal source from which the opinions in this book have been gleaned (and the illustrations reproduced). Therefore, a reasonably complete summary of their content should be my first obligation. No catalogue of these drawings yet exists, but that will take a competent bibliographer a long time to complete, since so many drawings are neither placed nor dated.

As has already been noted, the Lushington and the Northbrook collections, the largest aggregations of the nineteenth century, have furnished by far the greatest proportion of Harvard's holdings. Equally, Mr. William B. Osgood Field of New York was by far the principal benefactor, since he not only bought heavily from the Lushington inheritance but almost the whole of the Northbrook. The extent of this latter has probably not yet been realized, for it is largely housed in two great wooden cabinets, roughly five feet high by over four feet wide, each containing thirty-two drawers two feet wide and twenty inches deep, which were acquired after Mr. Field's book (and catalogue) went to press in 1932. Most of the approximately twenty-six hundred drawings they contain are mounted, but very few are matted. At the top each cabinet is lettered, "Sketches by Edward Lear"; the drawers are also lettered — eighteen with names of cities and districts in India and Ceylon, fourteen with various towns and parts of Italy, eleven "Corsica," eight "Albania," two "Constantinople," two "Palestine," one

"Egypt," one "Dalmatia," one "Nice and Cannes," one "Early Sketches," and five simply "Lord Northbrook," with dates ranging from 1850 to 1867.

Unfortunately, the drawings in the cabinets were not in order when Harvard received them from Mr. Field; the numbering on the drawings (by several hands, not only Lear's) is capricious and overlapping; and quite a few mounts contain more than one drawing, although each mat has, finally, only one number assigned to it. We know that Lear was in the habit of revising these numbers frequently as he sold, gave away, lost, or reclassified his working drawings. The result is chaotic! Perhaps Lord Northbrook's librarian began by being systematic, but in the end he (or she) was not. So even today we are uncertain whether Harvard possesses all the drawings that were once in these two cabinets.

By far the largest number of drawings, however — over fifteen-hundred — of those still kept in the cabinets represent scenes in India and Ceylon. These must have originally been sketched in 1873 and 1874, but a number were elaborated later in Italy, after Lear's return to San Remo, as is sometimes noted in their margins. Yet even in these notations, while Lear attempted by fits and starts to be methodical, he had no established order. A single numbered mount may contain up to eighteen small sketches, or several large drawings may have received the same number! This same observation is also true of all the other Northbrook landscapes, including the Italian drawings, which range in date mainly from 1837 to 1869. Of these there are over three hundred and fifty. Corsica (1868) is represented by three hundred and forty-nine drawings, Albania and Greece by over two hundred and fifty, and there are some scores of drawings from other parts of the Mediterranean basin. The early 1837 sketches drawn on Lear's first voyage to Italy by way of Luxembourg, Germany, and Switzerland number twenty-two. The grand total of landscapes in the Northbrook Collection, of various sizes and shapes, thus comes to about twenty-six hundred and fifty. (Approximate figures are usually given above because it is quite easy to count drawings differently just as Lear himself did. Does one evaluate nine sketches on a single piece of paper as nine drawings or as one large leaf of sketches? Furthermore, drawings have been pasted together; are they one drawing or separate drawings? The figures given are conservative ones: an enthusiastic cataloguer could have made them considerably larger.)

Then there are the early and middle-period landscape drawings from the Lushington collection which have been listed in the book edited by Mrs. Bertha Coolidge Slade for Mr. Field, *Edward Lear on My Shelves*. These consist of four hundred and ten numbered drawings ranging from a small pencil sketch, labeled "Burpham, October 3, 1834," done in Lear's youth in England, all the way to finished drawings done in Ceylon in 1874 and reworked in 1884, ten years later. This figure does not count the two hundred finished monochrome landscape drawings for Tennyson's *Poems* which Lushington also possessed and Mr. Field purchased after the Lushington sale, nor about one hundred and fifty landscapes and near landscapes contained in various scrapbooks. These last are hardest of all to enumerate, and neither Mr. Field nor Mrs. Slade made any real attempt to do so. Is a bird's nest with a naturalistic background of trees and flowers a landscape or a natural history study? I think it is the latter, as are all the drawings of birds, animals, shells, and flowers. Equally it seems to me that nonsense botanical drawings should be considered in that category, and not as "imaginative landscape scenes." Studies of trees are very hard to categorize, but they are here considered as natural history studies, and not landscapes. And what are landscape tracings, perhaps by Lear and perhaps not? In this case the answer is more obvious; they should not be counted. Excluding these questionable categories, the final estimate I have made of over three thousand four hundred landscape drawings in Harvard's possession is a very conservative one that can be easily supported. This number includes over fifty landscape drawings which I gave to Mr. Field in exchange for nonsense material subsequently also given to Harvard, but does not include nearly sixty drawings I have bought since our joint gift in 1942 and still in my possession. Some of these are included among the illustrations of this book because they represent subjects, places, and highly finished techniques not represented in Mr. Field's holdings. Unfortunately, Mr. Field notably lacked scenes in Greece because so many of these were bought soon after the Lushington and Northbrook sales by Mr. Gennadius and are now in Athens. Most of my Lear drawings and my few oils are of Greek subjects, intended to rectify this one unfortunate imbalance; but the price I have paid has made me regret having left all the landscape purchases to Mr. Field in the early 1930's, when they could be had for a song! Mr. Gennadius paid an average of five shillings each for his at London in 1930–31.

So much for Harvard's collection in some detail. It is not possible for me to be equally precise about other collections in the United States, since published statistics are lacking and drawings have been changing hands very rapidly. In any case, this is not the time nor the place for an exact census: only an indication is given for the reader's benefit. But he must realize that almost as soon as any figures are written down they may be out of date because of sales or gifts to other individuals and institutions.

At other public institutions in America there do not seem to be any considerable aggregations of Lear drawings except in the Henry E. Huntington Library and Art Gallery at San Marino, California, where there are thirty-six, mainly acquired in 1959 from the Gilbert Davis Collection in England. Princeton University has six drawings, and Yale University will shortly have at least

an equal number through the new (late 1966) gift of Paul Mellon's art collection and library. The Smith College Museum of Art has two fine drawings, one a rare study of trees in color. The Metropolitan Museum in New York has two, the Worcester Art Museum has one, and the Boston Museum of Fine Arts four. The Fogg Art Museum at Harvard has two, and there are probably a few scattered drawings in other art galleries and libraries throughout the country, but no group of any size that I have been able to discover.

A curator at Yale possesses a much larger collection than the University itself, Donald C. Gallup having probably more Lear landscape drawings than any other individual in the United States, with a total of over two hundred and eighty (mainly small views made in Egypt in 1867, he reports). He also has some very early scenes drawn in England and Italy between 1834 and 1838, and five oils. The late Ray Murphy's Lear landscapes (about thirty in number) were also at Yale for a period, but are now in his mother's house, as reported by his brother, Dr. James S. Murphy. Michael Coe, in New Haven, has five watercolors and three oils; Professor Beecher Hogan has four drawings, and there may be others near by.

At Princeton, Professor Charles Ryskamp, Gillett Griffin, E. T. Cone, Professor E. D. H. Johnson, and Professor William Shellman all have a few Lear drawings — proving, as in the case of the collections at Yale, that the interest of one collector is apt to encourage that of others.

This is also true in the Harvard area, although I do not think it was my example that spurred on either Robert S. Pirie in Hamilton, Massachusetts, or an anonymous collector in Cambridge who has twenty-eight landscapes! David McCord, a scholar and Lear enthusiast, has five very nice watercolor drawings in Boston. I have about sixty Lear drawings all told (nearly all large, including about twenty finished ones), and five oils.

New York, as would be expected, has a number of private collectors owning Lear drawings and sketches: Miss Jane Sommerich, Mr. and Mrs. Arnold Whitridge, Mrs. Robert M. Benjamin, Mr. and Mrs. Paul Sylbert, Mr. and Mrs. James Biddle, Mr. and Mrs. Cass Canfield, Mr. and Mrs. David Levine, Mr. and Mrs. Herbert Kaplan, Dr. and Mrs. J. S. Ritter, and George A. Dix, who has undoubtedly encouraged all the collectors in his vicinity and many at a distance through his long time interest in British art. W. K. Rose at Vassar College is not far away. In Providence, Rhode Island, Mrs. Murray S. Danforth has Lears, as has John Nicholas Brown. In Washington, J. Carter Brown and David Rust have also purchased Lear drawings in recent years.

But as far as I can easily ascertain, no very general interest in Lear as a landscape draughtsman has grown up in the Middle West or in the South. In the Far West, Francis P. Farquhar of San Francisco has several Lears. Certainly there must be other drawings there, and also in Los Angeles, thanks to the interest aroused by the Huntington Library's fine exhibition and illustrated catalogue of 1962.

Inevitably, however, it is still in England that the largest number of Lear drawings and oils continue to be found. But the problem of locating them has become increasingly difficult as the prices obtained in the sales rooms have mounted and the drawings themselves have changed hands. Many more institutions in the British Isles have Lear drawings than in America, but few have any large number of them. So far as I can determine, the City Library of Lincoln has the largest number at the moment, thanks to the deposit of the Tennyson Papers there, amongst which two hundred illustrations for the Poet Laureate's poems were recently found. (This was described by M. R. Bruce in *Country Life*, for October 8, 1964.) But while this is a very fine group of late drawings, it is not a diversified one such as Brian Reade has in his custody at the Victoria and Albert Museum in London — nearly one hundred sketches and drawings altogether, from early pencil sketches made in England in 1837 to drawings of the 1860's in the Near East and Greece. Surprisingly enough, this is about double the number of Lear landscapes in the British Museum, where only about fifty drawings are presently located, mainly of English and Italian subjects. The Ashmolean Museum at Oxford had fifty-four in 1965; but the Fitzwilliam Museum of Cambridge had only one, recorded in the Arts Council of Great Britain Exhibition of 1958, although they certainly have one other watercolor, and at least one great oil painting. The British Council itself has six Lear drawings. The Whitworth Art Gallery in Manchester has nine, mostly in color and of the Mediterranean basin, although one of their landscape drawings is an Indian subject. The Birmingham Museum of Art has one Greek drawing of 1849. The Tate Gallery in London has altogether twenty-five, the gift of Lord Northbrook in 1910. The Bolton Museum and Art Gallery has several good drawings, as does the Cecil Higgins Museum at Bedford. The City of Leicester Museums and Art Gallery have a fine Egyptian scene of 1854. And, finally, the National Gallery of Scotland in Edinburgh has one drawing. But this brief count may not include all public collections in the British Isles: there may well be some others who have not been reached or reported.

In the private sector, there are few large collections any longer, but there are again many more small ones than in America. A number of Lear drawings are always to be found if one hunts through the London dealers such as Colnaghi's, the Fine Arts Society, John Manning, the Leicester Galleries, Mrs. Robert Frank, Craddock and Barnard, and Agnew's. The latter at the moment of this writing (December, 1966) has fifty-two drawings, formerly belonging to Sir Osbert Sitwell, for Tennyson's *Poems*. As a guess, I would suppose at least fifty Lear drawings change hands every year, but with the very high prices now obtained, and the relative scarcity of important ones, this number may decline in future years. Lear is now definitely more expensive than his competitors (if we may call them that), David Roberts and J. D. Harding, William J. Müller, and John Frederick Lewis. Only Richard Dadd, who, after all, only took one trip to the Mediterranean area, is costlier, partly because much rarer, than Lear.

Madame Jean Morin, in Kent, has at least ten Lear drawings I am told; the Lord Tennyson, in the same county, has seven in addition to a proprietorship or perhaps the *sole* proprietorship of the Tennyson Papers and drawings now deposited in the City Library of Lincoln! The Lord Strachie, of Sutton Court, has six drawings and some oil paintings. His family holdings are among the oldest and best, since they stem directly from the artist himself. C. N. P. Powell of London had fifteen until recently when eight, very sadly, disappeared. The Lord Bridges, his daughter Mrs. T. H. Aston, and his son T. E. Bridges, have fifteen of various periods and countries. Stephen Harrison in London has nineteen drawings, while his relative David Markham, who lives at Lear Cottage in Sussex, has over a dozen. Edgar Behrens of Bradford has eight and his daughter one; Mrs. Robert Hollond has four; Mr. and Mrs. Osbert Lancaster have four; Ashley Ponsonby has several fine Greek ones; and I have no present record of how many the Harold Nicolson family own, although surely they have a number.

But still larger holdings are in a few very special hands, again running back for a long time. Members of the Hollis family and other descendants of Charles Marcus Church, a friend of Lear's, own or owned more than fifty drawings which were exhibited in 1964 by the Graves Art Gallery of Sheffield. Lieutenant-Colonel C. J. B. Church had then about a dozen, Sir Roger Hollis fourteen, and the Right Reverend Bishop Hollis eleven. Members of the Lubbock family, heirs of Sir John Lubbock (later the first Baron Avebury), one of Lear's principal patrons, are said to have quite a few, as also the heirs of Chichester Fortescue, later Lord Carlingford. The Earl of Derby, through his librarian at Knowsley, Mrs. Millett, has very kindly consented to allow me to report that he has "some parcels of Lear landscape drawings, and a number of folders containing original sketches," but that "there are neither thousands, nor hundreds of Edward Lear's works here." One would assume, however, that there may be at least several score. Sir Steven Runciman has at least forty-two, many of Greece, which are of the highest quality and interest. Peter Edwards, a collateral descendant of Lear, seems to have disposed of the bulk of his Lear drawings after the 1958 Arts Council Exhibition in London. It is reported from London that Franklin H. Lushington, who is often in Ceylon, still possesses five Lear drawings. But after naming these larger collections and families who may have considerable holdings of Lear landscape drawings, one is soon brought back again to those individuals in England who have only a few: L. G. Duke had about five quite recently unless these have now gone to Paul Mellon in America. The Earl of Perth has several. Dr. Joan Evans had three in the Arts Council Exhibition as also had Osbert Barnard personally. So had John Witt and Alan Ray Milburn, as witness the exhibition catalogue, though it is by no means certain that all these generous lenders do not have more. Dr. and Mrs. Francis Springell, who live in the English Lakes district, have a fine 1848 view of Athens. Charlotte, Lady Bonham Carter, has at least one, as have Angus Davidson, Lear's biographer, Julian Agnew, Professor Paul Thompson, Evelyn Joll, J. B. Kenricks, Lord Caccia, and Miss Spooner of Oxford.

Miss Mary Shaw of Haslemere has a number, since she is a member of the Strachie family. Miss Margaret Medley and her family have several, as has R. E. Abbott of London, while A. R. Skirving of Nottingham and J. Fairbank of Bradford have at least one apiece. John Rickett is said to have four, and Lady Rachel Labouchère had two of Corfu subjects in 1965. Captain Robert Gordon Canning, Eric Dunstan, the Reverend E. P. Baker (very possibly through the Church collection), and R. G. Searight, each have at least one, and John Mallett of the Victoria and Albert Museum has two, as has Clissold Tuely of Kent. Mrs. M. Jennings of Kent had two drawings in the Sheffield exhibition.

It is quite clear that with time and endless effort, I could have accumulated the names of many other British collectors and individuals who have Lears. But meanwhile this book would have been seriously delayed, and some of the owners would either have disposed of their drawings or added more, thus making this very general survey more suppositious than it already is! After all, my chief purpose is to show the range of distribution, the fact that there are more collections of Lear drawings still in England than in America, but that no collection there, outside of the few largest public ones, has a very large quantity. And this to me is the most significant fact: that with all the collections, public and private, in England and the British Commonwealth ranging only from several hundreds to one or two, there probably never were as many as "ten thousand large cardboard sheets of sketches," as stated by Hubert Congreve — even if one includes all the finished drawings, the drawings for Tennyson *Poems*, and most of the larger drawings counted separately, with "sheets" at Harvard and elsewhere considered as single items only where the drawings and sketches on them are quite small.

This rough estimate is supported by the meager statistics I have been able to gather easily on the Continent of Europe. In France, there is a fine Lear "gouache" in the Musée Condé at Chantilly, bought by that great nineteenth century French collector, the Duc d'Aumale. But the French do not know Lear at all well. Even in Greece, where there is one large and very fine public collection at the Gennadius Library of the American School of Classical Studies (over two hundred Lear landscape drawings, mainly Greek subjects), Francis Walton, its curator, informs me there are only a few sizeable collections — "the several scores" of Mrs. Maria Spentsa and probably smaller numbers in the possession of George Plytas, Evangelos Averoff Tossizza, Dr. J. Peristiany, Basil Mostras, George Seferiades, and Aristeides Pilavakis, who is now Greek Ambassador to Canada. Should the British School of Archaeology's drawings in Athens be called a British Collection or a Greek one? And how should one classify at least six drawings owned by Mrs. Alan Wace, a British subject living in Athens? Or those of Mark Ogilvie-Grant? Lambros Eutaxias has several oil paintings; he may also have some Lear landscape drawings or sketches as well.

Finally, what may there be in Germany, the Netherlands, Scottish private collections, Ireland, Spain, and other less likely European countries? There certainly should be a few Lears in Dalmatian cities, Istanbul, Jerusalem, and Cairo, because Lear spent considerable time in their vicinity. That there are drawings in Corfu is a near certainty, but the British Council Exhibition of 1964 did not reveal any helpful statistics. It would take untold months to canvas India and Ceylon. And the chances of finding any appreciable quantity would be very slight. It is nearly certain that the vast majority of drawings Lear made on his visit in 1873–74 went to Lord Northbrook, and are now at Harvard.

A Short Bibliography of Works Relating to Lear's Landscape Drawings

IX

Manuscripts by Edward Lear

Diaries (1858–1887 inclusive), 30 volumes.
Journals in India (1873–1875), 2 volumes.
Journal of a Voyage to Crete (4 April–4 May, 1864), one volume.

All of the foregoing are in the Department of Graphic Arts, Harvard College Library, Cambridge, Massachusetts. Some pen landscape drawings by Lear are contained in the Diaries. A number of other manuscript journals undoubtedly exist — some perhaps in New Zealand. Notebooks, too, must be in existence, also relating to Lear's landscape drawings.

Books by Edward Lear

Views in Rome and Its Environs. London: T. M'Lean, 1841. Illustrated with one half-page and 24 full-page tinted landscape lithographs by Lear. Some copies of this book have the lithographs colored by hand.

Illustrated Excursions in Italy. London: T. M'Lean, 1846. Illustrated with 30 full-page tinted landscape lithographs by Lear and 41 small monochrome wood-engraved landscape vignettes after Lear, engraved by various artists.

Illustrated Excursions in Italy. Volume II. London: T. M'Lean, 1846. Illustrated with 25 full-page tinted landscape lithographs by Lear and 13 small monochrome woodcut landscape vignettes after Lear, engraved by various artists.

Journals of a Landscape Painter in Albania and Illyria.

London: R. Bentley, 1851. Illustrated with 20 full-page tinted landscape lithographs by Lear.

Journals of a Landscape Painter in Southern Calabria. London: R. Bentley, 1852. Illustrated with 21 full-page tinted landscape lithographs by Lear.

Views in the Seven Ionian Islands. London: E. Lear, 1863. Illustrated with one half-page and 20 full-page tinted landscape lithographs by Lear.

Journal of a Landscape Painter in Corsica. London: R. J. Bush, 1870. Illustrated with 40 full-page and 40 small monochrome landscape woodcuts after Lear, by various artists.

Note: *Gleanings from the Menagerie and Aviary at Knowsley Hall* (Knowsley: privately printed, 1846) has some landscapes in the background, as does *Tortoises, Terrapins and Turtles* (London: H. Sotheran, etc., 1872).

Books, Essays, and Catalogues about Edward Lear

Tennyson, Alfred, Lord. *Poems.* London: Boussod, Valadon and Co.; New York: Scribner and Welford, 1889.
   (1) To Edward Lear, on his Travels in Greece
   (2) The Palace of Art
   (3) The Daisy
Introductory essay about Lear by Sir Franklin Lushington. Illustrated with 16 full-page and 6 vignette, monochrome photographic (gravure) reproductions of Lear landscape drawings. Limited to 100 copies.

Macmillan's Magazine (London), vol. 75, pp. 410–411 (April 1897): Essay in appreciation of Lear by F.L. (Sir Franklin Lushington).

Strachey, Lady Constance, editor. *Letters of Edward Lear.* London: T. F. Unwin, 1907. Illustrated with one full-page colored, 2 full-page tinted, and 9 full-page monochrome photographic reproductions of Lear landscape drawings and lithographs, as well as some small monochrome reproductions of sketches.

Strachey, Lady Constance, editor. *Later Letters of Edward Lear.* London: T. F. Unwin, 1911. Illustrated with one full-page colored, one full-page tinted, and 10 full-page monochrome photographic reproductions of Lear landscape drawings, paintings, etc.

Hardie, Martin. "Edward Lear." *Artwork* (London), No. 22 (Summer 1930), pp. 114–118.

Slade, Bertha C., editor. *Edward Lear on My Shelves* (for W. B. O. Field). New York: privately printed, 1933. Illustrated with 34 small, 16 large monochrome, and 5 large colored photographic reproductions of Lear landscape drawings.

Davidson, Angus. *Edward Lear.* London: J. Murray, 1938. Biography illustrated with 8 full-page monochrome photographic reproductions of Lear landscape drawings and paintings. Reissued as a paperback: Harmondsworth: Penguin Books (#747), 1950.

Proby, Granville. *Lear in Sicily.* London: G. Duckworth, 1938. Essay on a trip of J. J. Proby and Lear in 1847. Illustrated with one full-page colored photographic reproduction of a Lear landscape drawing.

Mégroz, R. L. "The Master of Nonsense." *The Cornhill Magazine* (London), vol. 157, no. 938 (February 1938), pp. 175–190 inclusive, esp. pp. 178–180.

Reade, Brian. *Edward Lear's Parrots.* London: G. Duckworth, 1949. No landscape reproductions, but some important references to Lear's talent.

Davidson, Angus, and Philip Hofer, editors. *Teapots and Quails . . . by Edward Lear.* London: J. Murray, 1953; Cambridge, Massachusetts: Harvard University Press, 1953. No landscape reproductions, but an Introduction and a Foreword with references to them.

Murphy, Ray, editor. *Edward Lear's Indian Journal.* London: Jarrolds, 1953. Illustrated with 9 full-page colored, 10 full-page and 2 half-page monochrome photographic reproductions of Lear landscape drawings.

Arts Council of Great Britain. *Edward Lear* (exhibition catalogue). London: Arts Council Gallery, July 1958. Foreword by Philip James; introduction by Brian Reade. Illustrated with 3 monochrome photographic reproductions of Lear landscape drawings.

Henry E. Huntington Library and Art Gallery. *Drawings by Edward Lear* (exhibition catalogue). San Marino, California, 1962. Introduction by R. R. Wark. Cover illustrated with reproduction of colored drawing and text illustrated with one large and 6 smaller monochrome photographic reproductions of Lear landscape drawings.

Hofer, Philip. *Edward Lear.* New York: Oxford University Press, 1962. Essay; illustrated with 4 half-page monochrome photographic reproductions of Lear landscape drawings.

Edward Lear in Southern Italy (mainly a reprint of Lear's *Journals of a Landscape Painter in Southern Calabria*). Introduction by Peter Quennell. London: William Kimber, 1964. Reproductions of 20 lithographs by Edward Lear from the original edition of 1852.

Durrell, Lawrence, editor. *Lear's Corfu, an Anthology Drawn from the Painter's Letters.* Preface by Lawrence Durrell. Corfu (Greece): Corfu Travel, 1965. Reproductions of 8 views of Corfu from Lear's lithographic originals in *Views in the Seven Ionian Islands*, 1863.

Edward Lear in Greece (mainly a reprint of Lear's *Journals of a Landscape Painter in Albania and Illyria*). Introduction and Publisher's Note (unsigned). Two maps. Reproductions of 20 lithographs by Edward Lear from the original edition of 1851.

General Works on Biography, Criticism, and English Art of Lear's Time

Price, Sir Uvedale. *Essays on the Picturesque.* London: Fr. J. Mawman, 1810. 3 volumes.

Thieme, Ulrich, and Felix Becker. *Allgemeines Lexikon der Bildenden Künstler,* etc. Leipzig, 1907–1950. 37 volumes, Completed by Hans Vollmer.

Clark, Kenneth. "On the Painting of English Landscape."

Proceedings of the British Academy, vol. XXI. London, 1935.

Allen, B. S. *Tides in English Taste (1619–1800)*. Cambridge, Massachusetts: Harvard University Press, 1937. 2 volumes.

Piper, John. *British Romantic Artists*. London: W. Collins, 1942.

Clark, Kenneth. *Landscape into Art*. London: J. Murray, 1949.

Musée de l'Orangerie, Paris. *Turner 1775–1851* (exhibition catalogue). Paris, 1948.

Oppé, A. P. *Alexander and John Robert Cozens*. London: Adam and Charles Black, 1952.

Williams, I. A. *Early English Water-Colours*. London: The Connoisseur, 1952.

Sutton, Thomas. *The Daniells, Artists and Travellers*. London: The Bodley Head, 1954.

Tooley, R. V. *English Books with Coloured Plates, 1790 to 1860, A Bibliographical Account*. London: B. T. Batsford, 1954.

Le Maitre, Henri. *Le Paysage Anglais*. Paris: Bordas, 1955.

Ritchie, A. C. *Masterpieces of British Painting 1800–1950* (exhibition catalogue). New York: Museum of Modern Art, 1956.

British Museum. *Eight Centuries of Landscape and Natural History in European Water Colour, 1180–1920* (exhibition catalogue). London, 1958.

Hewett, Osbert Wyndham, editor. *And Mr. Fortescue . . .* London: John Murray, 1958. A selection of passages from the diaries of Chichester Fortescue, Lord Carlingford, during the years 1851–1862.

Arts Council of Great Britain. *The Romantic Movement* (exhibition catalogue). London: The Tate Gallery, 1959. Introduction by Kenneth Clark, and other essays.

Walton, Francis R. "English Archaeological Drawings of the XVIIIth Century." *Hesperia*, vol. XXXI, no. 4. Athens: The American School of Classical Studies, 1962.

Taylor, Basil, and others. *Painting in England 1700–1850; The Collection of Mr. and Mrs. Paul Mellon* (exhibition and collection catalogue). Richmond, Virginia: Virginia Museum of Fine Arts, 1963. 2 volumes.

The British Council, London. ΕΝΤΟΥΑΡΝΤ ΛΗΑΡ. Corfu (Ionian Islands): Greece. Catalogue of an exhibition of watercolors, with a foreword by Angus Davidson. (May–June, 1964). The exhibition contained 48 Lear landscape drawings.

The Graves Art Gallery, Sheffield, England. Exhibition Catalogue, 1964, with Foreword by H.F.C., and notes by Michael Hollis (contains brief descriptions of 54 Lear landscape drawings).

Bruce, M. R. "A Portfolio of Monasteries: Edward Lear's Sketches of Mount Athos." *Country Life*, October 8, 1964. Article, with two illustrations from the newly rediscovered series of drawings for Tennyson's *Poems* deposited in 1963 by the Tennyson family in the City Library of Lincoln, England.

(Dimensions of originals are given in inches)

Zante, 1848 (1857). 11 1/2 x 18   *frontispiece*
Edward Lear *ca.* 1860, from a photograph taken in Rome
      facing p. 1

Plates

1. a. Pencil sketches, *ca.* 1830. 9 x 6 1/2
   b. Javanese Peacock, 1831. 9 x 7
2. *Illustrations of the Family of the Psittacidae,* 1832. 12 1/2 x 10
3. Antelope, 1832(?). 9 x 8 1/4
4. Burpham, October 3, 1834. 3 1/2 x 5 1/4
5. Umbrellifera, Kendal, August 20, 1836. 4 1/2 x 6 5/8
6. Rydal Water, October 7, 1836. 7 x 10 1/4
7. Luxembourg, July 20, 1837. 6 3/4 x 10
8. Frankfurt-am-Main, August 25, 1837. 11 x 7 1/2
9. Zürich, September 26, 1837. 10 x 14
10. Genzano di Roma, *ca.* 1837(?). 10 1/2 x 14 3/4
11. Tivoli, September 28, 1838. 12 x 17 1/2
12. Isola Farnese, April 1, 1840. 11 x 17 1/4
13. Nemi, October 12, 1840. 10 1/4 x 16 3/4
14. Trees, Italy, *ca.* 1840(?). 16 x 9 3/4
15. Rome: St. Peter's, *ca.* 1841(?). 11 1/4 x 17 1/4
16. Isola San Giulio, Lago di Orta, 1842. 9 3/4 x 13 1/2
17. Palermo, April 16, 1842. 9 1/2 x 16 3/4
18. Passerano, October 20, 1843. 7 3/4 x 15
19. Santa Rosa di Conca, June 8, 1844. 12 1/4 x 20 1/4
20. Amalfi, June 9, 1844. 17 1/4 x 10 3/4
21. Ponte Sant' Antonio, May 1, 1845. 11 1/4 x 19
22. San Vittorino, May 2, 1845. 11 x 18
23. Modica, June 7–8, 1847. 9 1/2 x 13 3/4

24. Melazzo, July 3, 1847. 14 x 19 3/4
25. Zante, April 30, 1848. 10 x 14 3/4
26. Athens, June 5–6, 1848. 11 1/2 x 19 3/4
27. Athens, June 5, 1848, evening. 11 1/4 x 17 1/2
28. Athens, July 23, 1848. 4 1/2 x 14 1/4
29. Between Chalcis and Castella, June 22, 1848. 8 1/4 x 17 3/4
30. Sweet Waters of Asia, September 1, 1848. 10 x 18 1/4
31. a. Constantinople, 1848. 3 1/2 x 6 1/2
    b. Beybek (Beylerbey), Bosphorus, 1848. 3 1/2 x 6 1/2
32. Gallipoli, September 10, 1848. 6 3/4 x 10
33. Ostrovo, September 15, 1848. 12 3/4 x 19 1/2
34. Akhrida, September 23, 1848. 13 1/4 x 20 3/4
35. Monastir, September 19, 1848. 8 1/4 x 11 1/2
36. Berat, October [14], 1848. 20 3/4 x 14 1/4
37. Apollonia, October 19, 1848. 12 1/4 x 20 3/4
38. Cairo, January 10, 1849. 12 1/4 x 19 3/4
39. Mount Sinai, 1849 (1869). 7 x 15
40. Mount Sinai, January 27, 1849. 12 1/2 x 19 1/2
41. Corfu, *ca.* 1849. 12 x 20 3/4
42. Leondari and Sparta, March 22, 1849. 10 x 16 1/2
43. Nemea, March 31, 1849. 7 x 10 1/2
44. Parga, May 7, 1849. 9 1/4 x 14 1/2
45. Baba (Tempe), May 18, 1849. 10 3/4 x 17
46. Scutari, October 4, 1849. 7 x 20 3/4
47. Thermopylae, 1848 (1863). 6 1/2 x 14 1/4
48. Mount Parnassus, *ca.* 1863(?) Oil. 9 1/4 x 14 3/4
49. Mount Olympus from Larissa, May 21, 1849. 11 x 20 1/2

50. a. Sir Richard Burton, December 23, 1853. 9 x 6
    b. Nile Scene, December 29, 1853. 5 3/4 x 9
51. Assouan, First Cataract, February 7, 1854. 13 x 19 3/4
52. Kôm Ombo, February 10, 1854. 12 1/4 x 19 3/4
53. Edfoo (Idfu), February 12, 1854. 11 1/4 x 19 3/4
54. Mount Athos, September 18, 1856. 13 1/2 x 21
55. Palaeocastritza, Corfu, December 12, 1856. 13 1/4 x 20 3/4
56. Janina, *ca.* 1861. 7 1/8 x 15
57. Petra, 1858. 9 3/4 x 15 1/4
58. Jerusalem, May 5, 1858. 7 x 20
59. Jerusalem, May 5, 1858. 6 1/2 x 20
60. Baalbek, May 23, 1858. 7 1/2 x 21 3/4
61. Corfu from Gasturi, 1862. 6 1/2 x 10 1/4
62. Palaeocastritza, Corfu, 1863. 13 1/2 x 22 3/4
63. Suda Bay, Canea, Crete, April 15, 1864. 14 x 21 1/4
64. Finale, Italian Riviera, December 16, 1864. 14 1/4 x 23
65. Finale, *ca.* 1878–83. 5 x 7 3/4
66. Sliema, Malta, December 30, 1865. 8 1/4 x 22
67. Sliema, Malta, March 1, 1866. 7 3/4 x 14 1/2
68. Cattaro (Kotor), April 29, 1866. 7 x 10 1/2
69. Cattaro (Kotor), *ca.* 1866. 6 1/2 x 10 1/4
70. Egypt, near Sugar Plantation, January 6, 1867. 5 1/2 x 9
71. Abou Simbel, February 8, 1867. 9 3/4 x 13 3/4
72. Forest of Bavella, Corsica, 1868. 11 1/2 x 18
73. a. Calvi, Corsica, 1868. 4 3/4 x 7 1/2
    b. Grosseto, Corsica, 1868. 5 x 7 3/4
74. Suez Canal, November 3, 1873. 6 1/4 x 13 3/4
75. Aden, November 12, 1873. 6 x 13 1/2

76. Darjeeling with Mount Kanchenjunga, January 18, 1874. 13 3/4 x 27 3/4
77. Darjeeling with Mount Kanchenjunga, January 18, 1874, later. 13 3/4 x 19 3/4
78. Agra: Taj Mahal, February 15–16, 1874. 13 1/2 x 19 1/2
79. Roorkee, March 20, 1874. 13 3/4 x 20
80. Poona: Spray of *Poinciana regia*, June 18, 1874. 8 1/4 x 13 1/4
81. Sholapur: Lotus plants, July 19, 1874. 8 3/4 x 11 1/4
82. Poona: River view, June 15 and 27, 1874. 14 1/2 x 21 1/4
83. Calicut, Malabar coast, October 21–22, 1874. 13 x 19 1/2
84. Barrackpur, India: Trees, December 29, 1873. 10 1/2 x 17
85. Hanwele, November 28, 1874. 12 3/4 x 19 1/4
86. Lake Lugano, August 17, 1878. 6 1/2 x 11
87. Lake Como: Villa Serbelloni, August 20, 1878. 6 1/2 x 11
88. Athens, June 12, 1848 (1882). 4 x 8 3/4
89. Muttra, India, March 4, 1874 (1882). 4 x 8 3/4
90. Assisi, September 6, 1883. 12 1/2 x 19 1/2
91. Assisi: Fiume Biaggio, September 6, 1883. 11 x 19 1/4
92. Monte Generoso, Switzerland, August 14, 1879. 12 1/2 x 9 3/4
93. Abetone, August 20, 1883. 13 x 19 3/4
94. a. Sheikh Abou Fodde, January 8, 1867 (1884). 3 3/4 x 7 1/4
    b. Ajaccio, *ca.* 1883. 4 3/4 x 7 1/4

95. Forest of Bavella, Corsica, *ca.* 1869(?) 4 5/4 x 7 3/4
96. Palaeocastritza, Corfu, *ca.* 1882. 5 1/4 x 10 1/4
97. Palaeocastritza, Corfu, 1885. 6 1/4 x 10 1/4
    Sweet is the color of cove and cave — The Sea Fairies*
98. Barrackpur, India, 1885. 6 1/4 x 10 1/4
    Stands in the sun, and shadows all beneath — Love and Death*
99. Capo S. Angelo, Amalfi, 1885. 6 1/4 x 10 1/4
    One showed an iron Coast — Palace of Art*
100. Lake Lugano, 1885. 6 1/4 x 10 1/4
    Girt round with blackness — Palace of Art*
101. Finale, Italian Riviera, 1885. 6 1/4 x 10 1/4
    What slender campanile grew . . . The Daisy*
102. Mount Athos, 1885. 6 1/2 x 10 1/4
103. Paestum, 1885. 6 1/4 x 10 1/4
104. Beachy Head, 1885. 6 1/2 x 10
    Between the steep cliff and the coming wave . . . Guinevere*
105. Coast of Travancore, India, 1885. 6 1/2 x 10
    A looming bastion fringed with fires — In Memoriam*
106. Olive Trees, 1858. Oil sketch. 18 x 23
107. Corfu from Ascension, *ca.* 1858. Oil. 15 1/4 x 9 1/2
108. a. Corfu citadel, 1849. 5 1/2 x 9 1/4
     b. Corfu citadel, *ca.* 1861. 2 1/2 x 3 3/4
     c. Ulysses island, off Corfu, 1861. 4 1/2 x 7 1/8
109. Petra, *ca.* 1870. Oil. 36 x 60

* The line from Tennyson "illustrated" by the plate.

a. Pencil sketches, *ca.* 1830.

b. Javanese Peacock, 1831.

ILLUSTRATIONS

of the Family of Psittacidæ

or

PARROTS

By E. LEAR, A.L.S.

Illustrations of the Family of the Psittacidae, 1832.
Detail of lithographic landscape.

Antelope, 1832(?).

Burpham, October 3, 1834.

Umbrellifera, Kendal, August 20, 1836.

Rydal Water, October 7, 1836.

Luxembourg, July 20, 1837.

Frankfurt – am – Main, August 25, 1837.

Zürich, September 26, 1837.

Genzano di Roma, *ca.* 1837(?).

Tivoli, September 28, 1838.

Isola Farnese, April 1, 1840.

Nemi, October 12, 1840.

Trees, Italy, *ca.* 1840(?).

Rome: St. Peter's, *ca.* 1841(?).

Isola San Giulio, Lago di Orta, 1842.

Palermo, April 16, 1842.

Passerano, October 20, 1843.

Santa Rosa di Conca, June 8, 1844.

Amalfi, June 9, 1844.

Ponte Sant' Antonio, May 1, 1845.

San Vittorino, May 2, 1845.

Modica, June 7–8, 1847.

Melazzo, July 3, 1847.

Zante, April 30, 1848.

Athens, June 5–6, 1848.

Athens, June 5, 1848, evening.

Athens, July 23, 1848.

Between Chalcis and Castella, June 22, 1848.

29

Sweet Waters of Asia, September 1, 1848.

a. Constantinople, 1848.

b. Beybek (Beylerbey), Bosphorus, 1848.

Gallipoli, September 10, 1848.

Ostrovo, September 15, 1848.

Akhrida, September 23, 1848.

Monastir, September 19, 1848.

Berat, October [14], 1848.

Apollonia, October 19, 1848.

Cairo, January 10, 1849.

Mount Sinai, 1849 (1869).

Mount Sinai, January 27, 1849.

Corfu, *ca.* 1849.

Leondari and Sparta, March 22, 1849.

Nemea, March 31, 1849.

Parga, May 7, 1849.

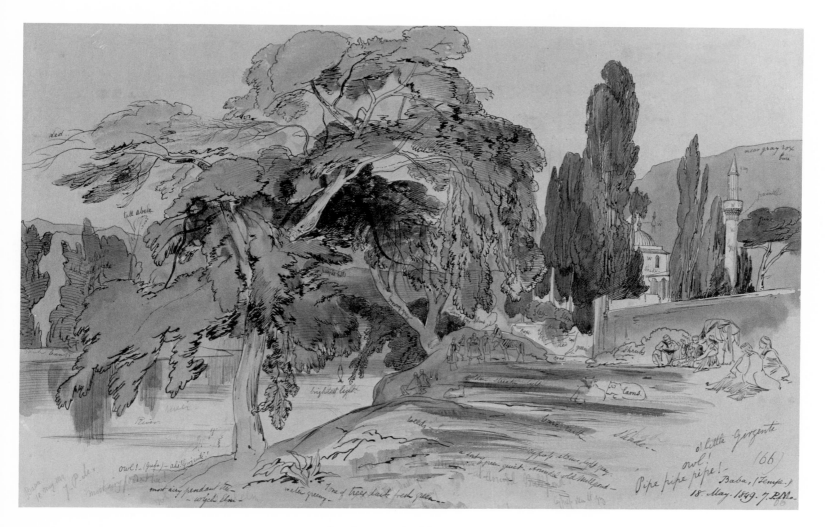

Baba (Tempe), May 18, 1849.

Scutari, October 4, 1849.

Thermopylae, 1848 (1863).

Mount Parnassus, *ca.* 1863(?) Oil.

Mount Olympus from Larissa, May 21, 1849.

a. Sir Richard Burton, December 23, 1853.

b. Nile Scene, December 29, 1853.

50

Assouan, First Cataract, February 7, 1854.

Kôm Ombo, February 10, 1854.

Edfoo (Idfu), February 12, 1854.

Mount Athos, September 18, 1856.

Palaeocastritza, Corfu, December 12, 1856.

Janina, *ca.* 1861.

Petra, 1858.

Jerusalem, May 5, 1858.

Jerusalem, May 5, 1858.

Baalbek, May 23, 1858.

Corfu from Gasturi, 1862.

Palaeocastritza, Corfu, 1863.

Suda Bay, Canea, Crete, April 15, 1864.

Finale, Italian Riviera, December 16, 1864.

Finale, *ca.* 1878–1883.

Sliema, Malta, December 30, 1865.

Sliema, Malta, March 1, 1866.

Cattaro (Kotor), April 29, 1866.

Cattaro (Kotor), *ca.* 1866.

8.30. A.M. Jan 6. 1867. near G. Sheikh Timai.

Egypt, near Sugar Plantation, January 6, 1867.

70

Abou Simbel, February 8, 1867.

Forest of Bavella, Corsica, 1868.

a. Calvi, Corsica, 1868.

b. Grosseto, Corsica, 1868.

73

(1)

Suez Canal. 3 Nov.ʳ 2 P.m. 1873.

Suez Canal, November 3, 1873.

Aden, November 12, 1873.

Darjeeling with Mount Kanchenjunga, January 18, 1874.

Darjeeling with Mount Kanchenjunga, January 18, 1874, later.

Agra: Taj Mahal, February 15–16, 1874.

Roorkee, March 20, 1874.

Poona: Spray of *Poinciana regia*, June 18, 1874.

Sholapur: Lotus plants, July 19, 1874.

Poona: River view, June 15 and 27, 1874.

Calicut, Malabar coast, October 21–22, 1874.

Barrackpur, India: Trees, December 29, 1873.

Hanwele, November 28, 1874.

Lake Lugano, August 17, 1878.

Lake Como: Villa Serbelloni, August 20, 1878.

Athens, June 12, 1848 (1882).

Muttra, India, March 4, 1874 (1882).

Assisi, September 6, 1883.

Assisi: Fiume Biaggio, September 6, 1883.

Monte Generoso, Switzerland, August 14, 1879.

Abetone, August 20, 1883.

a. Sheikh Abou Fodde, January 8, 1867 (1884)

b. Ajaccio, *ca.* 1883.

94

Forest of Bavella, Corsica, *ca.* 1869(?).

Palaeocastritza, Corfu, *ca.* 1882.

Palaeocastritza, Corfu, 1885.

Barrackpur, India, 1885.

Capo S. Angelo, Amalfi, 1885.

Lake Lugano, 1885.

Finale, Italian Riviera, 1885.

Mount Athos, 1885.

Paestum, 1885.

Beachy Head, 1885.

Coast of Travancore, India, 1885.

Olive Trees, 1858. Oil sketch.

Corfu from Ascension, *ca.* 1858. Oil.

a. Corfu citadel, 1849.

b. Corfu citadel, *ca.* 1861.

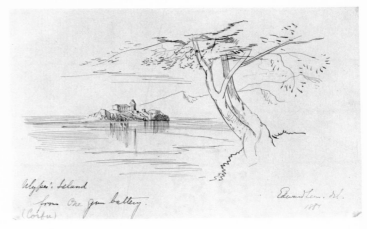

c. Ulysses island, off Corfu, 1861.

Petra, *ca.* 1870. Oil.

Two kinds of printing processes have been used in the production of this volume. The text portion was set on the Linotype and printed directly from type by the Harvard University Printing Office, and the illustrations were printed by photolithography under the direction of Harold Hugo at The Meriden Gravure Company. Both sections were printed on Mohawk Superfine paper.

The text type is Caledonia, designed by W. A. Dwiggins, and the captions are set in Fairfield Medium, designed by Rudolph Ruzicka. The binding is the work of Robert Burlen and Sons. Both the book and its jacket were designed by Gretchen Rosengren.